I0429530

Writings

10

Contributors:
Dr. Cesar D. Candari
Dr. Philip S. Chua
Percival Campoamor Cruz
Allen Gaborro
Ted Laguatan
Peter Alan Mariano
MLMunoz
Resty Odon
Alvin Tabanag

Tatay Jobo Elizes
Publisher, August 2011

Publisher
Tatay Jobo Elizes was born in Manila, Philippines, in 1934, retired businessman, now based in NY, busy writing and publishing as a hobby and involved in piglets dispersal programs for livelihood projects in the Philippines via the internet.

Acknowledgement
Gratitude and acknowledgment belongs to all who contributed their writings and those who encouraged me to continue publishing these writings book series.

Dedication
I dedicate this book to the **Filipino people**, and affectionately to my wife, **Cora**, my children, **Tetchie, Chevy & Abeth, and Marie & Bimbo,** my grandchildren, **Karines & Aung, Noelle, Chad, Marjo, Jeb, Marvin & Marty,** great-grandson **Jason Win** and my siblings **Susan, Hilda, Bobby, Bey & Manny** and to all my extended relatives.

ISBN-13-978: 1463728335
ISBN-10: 1463728336

Table of Contents

Foreword

Recorded words of authors become the mirrors of the times, and then in later years, as mirrors of history. Most specially when such words come out from famous persons in society, or from recognized writers and story tellers.

Most writers have only few articles and not enough to fill a book. The idea of collecting writings hit me. I myself have few materials. So, this Writings Book Series was born. Your ability to publish is solved in a nutshell. This can only be done with POD or Print On Demand, the new style in publishing. Under POD, this book will never be out-of-print for posterity. It's the best legacy to future generations. All contributing authors become easily searchable in the internet under books because of popularity of www.amazon.com, my host printer and online seller.

Why put writings in a book? And not just in the internet? It's all a matter of choice. Convenience is the name of the game. This book will always be there among your book collections or in libraries. Not everybody use the internet. I'm sure you, as an author, need wide readership. Internet access has its technical problems. One must have computers and elecronic gadgets to access and read. Not so with books. I still believe that a book is the best repository of writings. But my kindle editions of these books are also useful.

I just learned in my retired years that I have to find something that I really care about. Publishing is one and giving piglets is two. With little royalty from books, it helps a little to accomplish my goals. When authors consented to lend me their articles, and when book lovers buy my titles, in effect they are helping my cause unknowingly. I hope you get something or get a sense of history and events occurring before your very eyes by reading my books.

1

The Spratlys Are Worth Dying For

Ted Laguatan

Dateline, June 2011
First published at Inquirer.Net
No Limitations

(In line with the important campaign to make Filipinos and the whole world aware of what Spratlys is all about - and its significance to a brighter future for Filipinos - please disseminate far and wide and ask recipients to do likewise. Thanks.)

[Note: The California State Bar honors Atty. Ted Laguatan as one of the best lawyers in the US. He is one of only 29 lawyers officially certified as an Expert Specialist continuously for more than 20 years. He also does accident injuries, wrongful death and complex litigation. For communications: (San Francisco area): 455 Hickey Blvd. Suite 516, Daly City,Ca 94015 Tel 650-991-1154 Fax 650-991-1186.]

Email laqubatanlaw@gmail.com

The Spratly Islands is an archipelago of 750 small islands, islets, cays, reefs and atolls widely scattered off the coasts of Malaysia, the Philippines and Vietnam. It has a total land area of only about four square kilometers where hardly anything grows that's of significant value.

While these real estate may appear worthless, beneath are vast deposits of gold — black gold — oil. Natural gas is also present in huge quantities as evidenced by the Malampaya example.

The Philippines, Vietnam, Malaysia and Brunei are

claiming those portions of the Spratlys — which are within what is referred to by the 1982 United Nations Convention Law of the Sea (UNCLOS) as their Exclusive Economic Zone — an area within a 200 mile radius from a country's baseline.

On the other hand, China is claiming everything — those inside other countries' territories as well as those outside. While China is a signatory to this 1982 agreement among nations, its energy needs are recklessly driving the dragon into seeking to grab oil and natural gas that belong to other countries — the Philippines included.

Seventy percent of China's present oil needs is imported, mainly from Russia and the rest from other sources. The reality of being hostage to the demands of suppliers or the risk of disruption of continuous supply threatens China's astounding growth as an economic powerhouse.

Industries and manufacturers throughout the world have found it more advantageous and practical to farm out their production needs to China. Not only does this result in lower production costs, absence of labor problems and no management issues — it enables companies to focus on marketing operations which results in more profits.

The Chinese deserve much credit for coming out with quality products that sell cheaper. Great for consumers everywhere. The new prosperity is also good for the Chinese people — notwithstanding that much of the new wealth has yet to trickle down to the masses — which hopefully will happen over time.

The Chinese people deserve a better life after years of poverty and suffering from the excesses of the Cultural Revolution.

China's owes much of its booming economy to former Premier Deng Xiaoping who ditched rigid closed communist policies in favor of free market reforms.

The future looks very bright for the Chinese people. The planet's fastest growing economy has now surpassed Japan as the second largest economy in the world. As more companies look to farming out their production needs to China and Chinese companies expand their operations — expectedly its need for oil and energy resources will continue to increase.

However, this need does not justify grabbing the oil and natural resources belonging to smaller countries in the region and using brute force — which China appears ready to do. If China proceeds with its gorilla tactics, it will be viewed as a bully and as a thief by the global community. Its government will lose the respect of other nations, cause unrest and instability in the region and foment much continued resentment among the victim nations.

These negatives for China will have serious consequences including the threat of war against several countries — including even possibly against the United States whose interest is stability in the region as well as non disruption of its commercial regional activities here. If China's image of being untrustworthy and a bully escalates — not only will it deprive itself of valuable international goodwill — other countries might also ally themselves into a united front against Chinese abuse of power and for self defense.

On June 26, 2011, aware of the repeated forced intrusions into Philippine, Vietnamese and other countries' maritime territories, the US Senate unanimously passed a resolution condemning China's use of force to intimidate it's smaller neighbors as well as affirming the US resolve to use military force if need be to contain China.

China is a goliath with a population of around 1.3 billion people. It has the world's largest military force with 2.3 million soldiers. It also has nuclear capabilities, a formidable navy and air force. It can easily carry out a successful grab of the oil and natural gas resources of Vietnam, Malaysia, the Philippines and other countries.

These countries do not have the military capabilities to face up to China. In 1988, a contingent of Vietnamese sailors who tore down Chinese flags and buoy markers in part of the Spratlys which were within Vietnam's Exclusive Economic Zone — were slaughtered by Chinese gunboats using 37 mm cannons. Video records of this episode may be seen on YouTube. The Vietnamese were not fighting when deadly firepower was used on them. Some 66 Vietnamese sailors were killed.

The US stepping into the picture to preserve the balance of power and maintain geopolitical stability is much welcomed by countries in the region. Only the American eagle can neutralize the Chinese dragon.

For the Philippines, why are the Spratlys worth dying for?

China's official state news agency Xinhua reported a few weeks ago that around $30 billion will be invested in building modern oil drill platforms. An ultra advanced platform costing almost a billion dollars has just been completed and ready for transport to the drilling site this July. It is suspected that this site is in Philippine UNCLOS territory as the Philippines' previous president allowed the Chinese to freely explore these waters for oil searches during her term.

In talks with Foreign Affairs Secretary Albert Del Rosario, China insists that all of the Spratlys are theirs including those clearly within Philippine territory — and that their claim is non-negotiable. This bold assertion means that they put a very high value on those parts of Spratlys inside Philippine territory and appears from their actuations that they are willing to use force if need be.

Xinhua confirms that the target is to drill in 800 locations in the South China Sea (renamed by the Philippines as West Philippine Sea) — but does not specify where. The projected production is equivalent to $50 billion annually.

If a big part of such wealth goes to its rightful owners, the Filipino people — mass poverty can likely be eliminated. New industries and enterprises will proliferate from the infusion of so much national capital providing well paying jobs for our people. No longer will we be a nation of slaves where millions of our people have to work in lonely far away foreign lands separated from their families.

The superior education, nutrition, health care and housing these discovered riches will provide to millions of Filipino children will enable them to flower to their fullest potential.

China's intrusion into Philippine territory to take this promise of a brighter future from the Filipino people should be resisted with everything that we can muster — with blood if necessary. China's use of force to take away our oil for free must be condemned in no uncertain terms and brought to the attention of the world. If they want our oil, they should pay fair prices for it — not steal it.

The Philippines' claim is based on existing law agreed upon even by China and the other countries in the region

— the UNCLOS. The target sites for oil well drillings are also roughly about 100 miles more or less from Philippine shores whereas these are around a thousand miles from Chinese shores.

China's claim is based on an absurdity. Supposedly, an ancient map from the Han Dynasty about 2000 years old — defined the limits of the Chinese kingdom which includes all of the West Philippine Sea and surrounding lands. This self proclaimed right to distant other country owned territories has neither rhyme nor reason — legally speaking.

Assuming such a genuine map existed, that claim is about as valid as the Italian government claiming ownership of most of Europe, parts of Africa and parts of Asia because these were once all part of the Roman empire. The Roman empire ceased to exist hundreds of years ago — and so did the Han dynasty. Country boundaries keep changing over time because of various factors that I need not go into.

We must also be aware that China is not limiting its options to using force in seeking to acquire our energy resources. We should face up to the gruesome reality that many of our leaders and politicians are thieves and are so corrupt and willing to give all kinds of concessions to China (as well as to other private investors) for personal gain.

In 2004, then President Gloria Macapagal Arroyo signed a tripartite agreement with China and Vietnam known as the Joint Marine Seismic Undertaking (JMSU) involving seismic exploration of 142,866 square kilometers west of Palawan. More specifically, it is an agreement between the Philippine National Oil – Exploration Corporation (PNOC-

EC), China National Oil Offshore Corporation (CNOOC) and Vietnam Oil and Gas Corporation (PetroVietnam).

The problem with this agreement is that all of the area to be explored is within the Philippines' 200 mile Exclusive Economic Zone under UNCLOS including areas not even claimed by China or Vietnam. It hardly makes sense to expose one's wealth to countries that may be aiming to get it without respecting the Philippines' ownership rights. It's like showing the fox where the chickens are hidden. It does not include explorations outside Philippine waters.

Under this JMSU agreement, Chinese vessels would conduct the exploration, Vietnam would process the data gathered and the Philippines' PNOC would interpret the results. The explorations were supposed to end in January 2008 but there is no confirmation that it did.

What Barry Wain confirms about the JMSU is that "it was largely a sellout on the part of the Philippines". Wain is a respected Singapore based researcher for the Institute of Southeast Asian Studies. In an article he wrote for the widely read Hong Kong journal Far Eastern Economic Review, he said:

"The Philippines has made breathtaking concessions in agreeing to the areas of study including parts of its continental shelf not even claimed by China and Vietnam."

It appears from some accounts that Vietnam was hesitant to join the agreement but may have been included later on after Arroyo gave a 100 percent ok to China's exploration — probably to make the China-Philippine deal look more palatable and legitimate.

Arroyo critics suspect she entered into secret deals with the Chinese in return for $2 billion in loans for Philippine projects including the ZTE Broadband deal and others in which she and her husband are alleged to have received millions in equivalent US dollars of kickback. This would be a clearcut case of treason if such were the case.

The Malampaya Natural Gas project is also another blatant example of how our leaders sell out our precious natural resources. The share of the Philippines for the profits is only 10 percent whereas Chevron and Shell will split the rest of the 90 percent. There is not even an agreement for a transfer of technology later. Any fool can see that this is hardly a fair agreement.

The same anomalies and distortions have happened in providing mining rights to foreigners and local investors.

Perhaps in a very real way, President Benigno Aquino III may be a real blessing to the country. He may have some weak points but I strongly believe that he is not greedy, dishonest or corrupt — unless proven otherwise. I do not think he will betray the legacy of his martyred father and sincere mother who tried their best to serve the people.

If he is able to successfully defend the vast oil and natural gas resources of the country against military forces from the outside and from the corrupt elements within — and use this tremendous wealth to drastically improve the lives of so many of our people — he might become truly a really great president.

2

Ang Siyam Na Buhay Ni Felizardo Cabangban

Percival Campoamor Cruz

(Si Percival Campoamor Cruz ay nagtapos ng Masters in Business Admininistration (MBA) sa University of the Philippines; nasa pamatnugutan ng Philippine Collegian at The Guilder. Nagwagi ng unang gantimpala, maikling dula, *"Kalupitan ng Nakararami"*, 1963 Andres Bonifacio Centennial sa pagtangkilik ng Lungsod ng Maynila. Naging advertising executive ng Delta Motor Corp. (Toyota) - Reach, Inc. Lumikha ng mga newspaper, radio-TV ads para sa Toyota, Philippine Charity Sweepstakes Office, Philippine National Bank, Frigidaire, Hooven Aluminum, Zest-O, Mariwasa Tiles, Sharp, Pacific Memorial Plan, Sinclair Paint, at marami pang ibang institusyon at produkto. Producer, chief writer ng humigit-kumulang na dalawang-daang telenobela na lumabas sa Channels 2, 4, 7, 13 sa Pilipinas sa ilalim ng mga sumusunod na TV show titles - *"Sa Paghawi ng Tabing"* (host: Jaime dela Rosa); *"Quiapo"* (host: Eddie Rodriguez); *"Hiyas"* (host: Rio Locsin). Naging columnist ng Manila Bulletin *("Business Travel")* sa ilalim ng pamamatnugot ni Cornelio de Guzman. Kasalukuyan ay naninirahan sa Burbank, California at sumusulat ng mga maiikling kuwento para sa Asian Journal, ang pinakatanyag na pahayagan sa Amerika para sa Pilipino. He just published a book, **May Bagwis Ang Pag-ibig**, a collection of Tagalog short stories by himself and his father, under Tatay Jobo Publishing.)

Mahina ang tuhod ng matandang lalaki kung kaya't siya'y nakatalaga sa isang *wheelchair*. Nguni't bukod sa nasabing kapansanan ay wala nang iba pang karamdaman ang pitongpu't isang taong gulang na *residente* ng Sunflower Retirement House. Kay talas pa ng kanyang isip at malalakas pa ang kanyang mga bisig. Sa edad na iyon ay buo pa ang kanyang mga ngipin at malinaw pa ang paningin. Ayon sa doktor, ang kanyang puso ay masigla ang kabog at tila puso ng binata!

Ang matatandang katulad niya ay karaniwang nag-iisa na sa buhay at walang kamag-anak na nag-aalaga; sila'y nagiging *"pasyente"* sa tahanan ng matatanda, na kung saan, ay may upahang tagapag-alaga sila, may pribadong silid-tulugan, may pagkain, may pagpapa-araw sa tuwing umaga, may oras para sa panonood ng TV at pakikipag-usap sa mga kasamahang *"pasyente"* rin.

Ang matandang lalaki ay naroroon, itinalaga ng gobyerno, "upang siya ay maging malusog, maligaya, at ligtas sa kapahamakan."

"Bull-shit ang lahat ng `yan!*"* himutok ng matanda.

Maagang napag-alaman ng mga magulang ni Felizardo Cabangbang na ang kanilang anak ay isang masuwerteng nilalang. Kung di ba naman ay sumulpot siya sa mundo na may nakapulupot na kurdon ng pusod sa kanyang leeg! Karaniwang ang isinisilang sa gayong kalagayan ay nasasakal habang lumalabas sa sinapupunan ng ina, at patay na kung iluwal. Nguni't naiiba ang sanggol na ito.

Kung kaya't sa laki ng tuwa at pasasalamat ng mga magulang ay mabilis na pinabinyagan ang sanggol. At doon siya dinala sa parokya ng Santo Ninyo upang mabinyagan; ang mag-anak ay taga-Tundo. Felizardo ang piniling pangalan para sa kanya, bilang alaala sa ama ng ama, na Felizardo din ang pangalan, na ang ibig sabihin ay, Kagalakan.

Nang si Felizardo ay tumuntong sa edad na lima , ipinasok siya ng ina sa *kindergarten school* na naroroon sa bakuran ng parokya. Minsang naglalaro si Felizardo kasama ang mga kaeskwela, sa may gilid ng simbahan, isa sa mga bata ang nagpatigil sa kanilang paglalaro, at hinimok sila na sundan siya, patungo sa hardin ng eskwela. At nang makarating sila doon sa kalagitnaan ng malawak na hardin, na walang gusali sa paligid, sa walang kaginsa-ginsa, ay yumanig ang lupa. Lindol, lindol! Naghiyawan ang mga guro, habang nagtatakbuhan sila na litong-lito kung saan lilikas.

May malalaking tipak ng bato na napilas mula sa tore ng simbahan, sanhi ng malakas na pag-ugoy ng lupa, at bumagsak ang mga ito doon mismo sa dating pinaglalaruan ng mga bata. Kung hindi nilisan ng mga bata iyong lugar na iyon ay tiyak na may nabagsakan ng bato at may namatay sa kanila; marahil, ay si Felizardo.

Makalipas ang kahindik-hindik na lindol ay nagmisa ang kura-paroko bilang pasasalamat sa Diyos. Sa naturang misa ay napaupo ang mag-anak na Cabangbang sa dakong harapan ng simbahan, malapit sa altar, na kung saan nakalantad ang imahen ng Santo Ninyo. Natunghayan ni Felizardo ang Santo Ninyo; nanlaki ang mga mata niya, sumampa sa ina at nanggigilalas na ibinulong ang ganito: "Inay, inay", sabay turo sa Santo Ninyo, "siya . . . siya ang batang nagpasunod sa amin, bago lumindol!"

Kung may mga taong malas, ay isa marahil si Felizardo sa iilan na laging masuwerte. Nang nasa *high school* na, ay kinagat siya ng isang asong-kalye, habang naglalakad pauwi mula sa paaralan. Sa awa ng Diyos ay hindi siya nagkaroon ng *rabies*. Tiyak na pagkabaliw at kamatayan ang nagiging epekto ng *rabies*.

Muntik din siyang mabagsakan ng isang mabigat na bagay, nang ang isang aparador ay tumumba, sanhi ng malakas na hangin na pumalo sa bahay nila isang gabing natutulog si Felizardo sa sahig. Bumagsak at kumalabog sa sahig ang natumbang *mueble de madera* at, isang himala, hindi tinamaan ang ulo ni Felizardo, kahi't na ang pagitan mula sa natumbang aparador at sa ulo niya ay isang dangkal lamang! Kay lapit na kamatayan, na ang pagiging masuwerte lamang ang naging hadlang.

Minsang nagdiwang ng kaarawan si Felizardo ay binigyang-aliw siya ng ama. Isinama siya sa Calle Ongpin, na kung saan kumain sila ng *pata tim*, sa Panciteria San Jacinto. Sumakay sila, pagkatapos, sa isang *jeepney* at nagpahatid sa Baclaran at doon ay naglakad at nagpahangin sa may baybay-dagat. Bago umuwi ng bahay ay bumili ng isang banig ng loterya ang ama, na si Felizardo ang pumili, mula sa isang tindera na matiyagang bumuntot sa mag-ama sa kanilang paglalakad. Nang tingnan ng ama ang nanalong numero sa pahayagan, kinabukasan, napag-alaman niya na tumama ang kanyang taya. Ang salapi mula sa panalo ay siyang ipinagpatayo ng ama ng isang bagong bahay sa karatig na pook ng Maynila.

Nang maging ganap nang tao si Felizardo ay nag-*apply* siya ng trabaho sa isang *merchant shipping company* at natanggap naman kaagad. Ang barko, na kung saan siya ay nabigyan ng trabaho, ay naglayag sa pagitan ng Maynila at Los Angeles , California . Minsang ang barko ay papalapit sa daungan sa Long Beach, ay nagkaroon ng sunog sa *engine room*, nagkaroon ng malaking pagsabog, kumalat ang sunog sa buong barko at naglundagan sa dagat ang mga tripolante, kasama na si Felizardo.

Sampu sa mga kasamahan ni Felizardo ang naglaho sa sunog o sa dagat, dala ng pagkalunod. Sa kabilang dako, nakayanan ni Felizardo na lumutang sa tubig, sa tulong ng isang *salva-vida*, hanggang sa siya ay matagpuan at mailigtas ng *coast guard*.

Nagbitiw si Felizardo sa trabaho sa dagat at nanatili na lamang sa lupa. Nagpasiya siyang magpirmi sa siyudad ng Los Angeles , at doon ay makipagsapalaran. Walang tigil ang kanyang pagpupunyagi, at sa huli, siya ay nakahanap ng trabaho sa army. Di malaon ay nakapag-asawa siya ng isang kapuwa taga-Pilipinas, at namuhay sila nang matahimik at nakaririwasa, at napabilang sila sa mga taga-Pilipinas na iginalang bilang masisipag at mararangal na *naturalized Americans.*

Nang sumiklab ang *guerra* sa Vietnam , naatasan si Felizardo na maging *infantryman,* at siya'y ipinadala sa Saigon . Maliit na lalaki si Felizardo, nguni't gahigante ang kanyang katapangan. Napabalita ang kabayanihan niya, hindi ayon sa kanyang sariling salaysay, kundi ayon sa salaysay ng mga kasamahan sa *guerra*. Sa isang *encuentro*, sinabing may tama na ng bala si Felizardo sa kanyang kaliwang bisig; nguni't sa dahilang ang kanyang pangkat ay nasukol na ng mga sundalong Vietcong, ay di niya inalintana ang sugat at matapang na pinangunahan ang pagsagupa sa mga kalaban.

Pinulot ng mga kasamahan at ng *medic* si Felizardo na wala nang malay, dulot ng pagkawala ng maraming dugo. Inilikas siya sa isang ligtas na lugar, at pagkatapos ay isinakay sa isang Huey helicopter papunta sa ospital. Sa ika-anim na pagkakataon sa kanyang makulay na buhay, si Felizardo ay nanaig na naman sa hatak ng kamatayan. Ayon sa salaysay ng kanyang mga kapangkat, tila asong-ulol si Felizardo na sumugod sa pugad ng mga sundalong Vietcong, habang walang patlang na pinapuputok ang kanyang armas at inihahagis ang sunud-sunod na granada sa kumpol ng mga kalaban, hanggang sa mapatay niya silang lahat, na napag-alaman, pagkatapos, na isang pangkat na labing-pitong tao pala ang bilang.

Naging pangalawang bayan ni Felizardo ang Amerika. Binigyan siya nito ng parangal, bilang isang bayani. Matagal niyang pinag-isipan ang kung saan siya maninirahan: sa Pilipinas ba o sa Amerika. Laging nananariwa sa kanyang alaala ang alindog ng kanyang bayan at ang tamis ng pagmamahalan at pakikipagsamahan ng mga kamag-anak at kababayan sa sinilangang lupa. Iba ang simoy, ang himig, ang lasa, ang kulay at sayaw ng buhay sa Pilipinas. Mas masarap, mas masaya.

Nalulungkot siya sa tuwing maaalaala ang naiwang mga magulang; na sa kanilang pagtanda ay wala siya sa kanilang piling upang kumalinga sa kanilang mga pangangailangan. Ang mga kapatid na nakapag-asawa na at nagkaroon na ng mga anak at apo ay larawan ng tagumpay at kaligayahan na malimit niyang nakikita sa kanyang isipan – at nagdurugo ang kanyang puso na di niya nakita at nadama ang mahahalagang pangyayari sa buhay ng kanyang mga kamag-anak.

Nguni't pinakamahapdi ang alaala ni Estrella, ang kanyang naging kasintahan, na naghintay nang naghintay sa kanyang pagbabalik, hanggang sa siya'y nawalan na ng pag-asa, at sa huli, ay pumayag na mapakasal sa isang lalaking hindi lubos ang kanyang pagmamahal. Tayo'y may kalayaan, nguni't higit na malakas ang tawag at hatak ng kapalaran. Natiyak ito ni Felizardo sa sarili, habang nagbubulay-bulay tungkol sa kanyang nakalipas.

Nagugunita ni Felizardo ang paksa ng isa sa mga tulang isinulat ng kanyang makatang ama:

"TADHANA
habang minamasid
ang yukod ng sanga
at ang pagkalagas ng dahong nalanta
na wari'y hinabol
ng mga talulot
na pinigtal na rin ng hanging nagdala,
hindi ko mawari
ang hiwagang ito ng Katalagahang
siyang nagbabadya.
tanong sa sarili:
ang Tagsibol kaya'y nagtakda ng hangga
upang itong kulay, halimuyak, ganda'y
masarili niya?

kung saan hahantong
ang lagas na dahon
saka ang talulot na dinapit-hapon,
sa pakiramdam ko,
ang dibdib ng lupa ay sumasalubong,
gaya ng pagtanggap sa isang kabaong.
ngayon, ang sabi ko:
Tadhana! Sino ba ang makahahadlang
sa ibig mangyari

ng Katalagahan? . . .
kung ang Tagsibol, kay tuling nagdaan,
mahihintay nati'y ang isang Tag-ulan!
ulan ay luha rin ng Sangkatauhan
bendita ng langit
sa nahihirapan."

Ang huling pagsasaya ni Felizardo ay naganap sampung taon bago siya napapunta sa *retirement home.* Nilakbay niya ang kahabaan ng Interstate 5, mula sa San Diego hanggang sa Vancouver, na nag-iisa, sakay ng isang Harley-Davidson. -- Ang maglakbay nang nag-iisa, tungo sa saan mang ibig mong patunguhan, sa bilis na ang hangin ay humahampas sa iyong mukha at katawan, iyan ang ideya ko ng kalayaan, -- sambit ni Felizardo sa sarili.

Ginaygay niya ang *freeway,* at sa ilang lugar ay pumasok siya sa mga *country roads* at doon ay binusog niya ang kanyang mga mata sa magagandang tanawin sa may baybayin ng Dagat Pacifico at sa mga bulubunduking maliliit na bayan na malapit sa Monterey. Hinintuan niya ang maliliit na kapihan at nakipagkilala sa mga kapuwa *bikers* na ang edad ay kalahati lamang ng edad niya.

Pagsapit sa hangganan ng California at Oregon ay pinatakbo niya ang kanyang motorsiklo na pagkatulin-tulin na sumibat siya sa daan na parang isang umaapoy na demonyo.

Umuulan at madulas naman ang daan, pagsapit niya sa Washington; nguni't bale wala ang siya'y "matunaw" sa ulan; tila siya bata na hiyaw nang hiyaw at halakhak nang halakhak, habang sumisibat sa kalagitnaan ng sigwada sa mahabang *freeway* ang kanyang motorsiklo. Nagugunita niya ang isang payo ni Dalai Lama - *dance like nobody was watching you!*

Tila baga laging si Felizardo ay sinusundan ng sakuna at suwerte - may pinasok siyang isang *one-way* pala na daan, hindi niya namalayan, at nakipagsalpukan siya sa isang dumarating na *auto.* Ang tsuper na babae ay di inaasahang may masasalubong siya na motorsiklo. Dapat ay iyon na ang sakunang ikinamatay ni Felizardo, nguni't liban sa pagkabali ng buto sa kapuwa tuhod at binti, ay nakaligtas pang muli ang matibay na lalaki.

Walang halaga kay Felizardo ang dinanas na sakit sanhi ng pagkakaopera ng tuhod. Bale wala ang pagkawala ng kakayahang makalakad - mula noon ay magiging bilanggo na siya sa loob ng isang *wheelchair.* Ang higit na makirot at nakapagpalumo kay Felizardo ay ang pasiya ng pulisya na bawiin na ang kanyang *driver's license.* Matandaan na raw siya at di na maaaring makapagmaneho. Kapag nagmaneho pa ay magiging peligro siya sa kanyang sarili at sa ibang tao, sabi ng pulisya. At kaakibat ng pagkawala ng lisensiya sa pagmamaneho ay ang pagkawala ng kalayaan.

Pakiramdam niya ay preso siya sa loob ng isang maliit na bilangguan, ang *wheelchair;* at preso rin siya sa loob ng mas malaking kulungan: ang *retirement home.*

Nagbabalik sa kanyang alaala ang tahanan niya sa Los Feliz, sa kalagitnaan ng Los Angeles - isang karaniwang *three-bedroom* na *Victorian* ang *design.* Dalawangpu't- limang taong yaon ang naging maliit na paraiso ni Felizardo at ng kanyang kabiyak na si Elizabeth sa balat ng lupa. Aliw na aliw sila sa hardin na nasa likuran ng bahay, na siksik sa mga tanim na rosas at sampagita, at sa gilid-gilid, sa tanim na kamatis, ampalaya at kalamansi. Mayroon din silang malaking hawla ng ibon na pugad ng walong pares na *lovebirds* na sari-sari ang kulay. Bukod sa mga ibon ay mayroon silang alagang aso na pagkalambing-lambing sa kanila, na sa gabi ay natutulog pa sa paanan ni Felizardo.

Ang maybahay ay buhos ang pag-aalaga kay Felizardo, lalo na sa pagluluto. Ang pagkain ay ayon sa kanyang panlasa - pinakbet, sinigang na manok, kare-kareng baka na may sangkap na bagoong-isda; mga pagkaing nagpapaalaala sa kanya sa kanyang nakalipas na kabataan at sa yumao niyang napakabuting ina na napakasarap kung magluto. Kahi't sila'y dadalawa, at sila lamang ang laging magkasama sa bahay, ay di sila nagsasawa sa isa't isa at sa mga gawain sa araw-araw; at ang pagsasalo sa hapag-kainan, kahi't na karaniwang pangyayari lamang, ang pakiwari nila ay piging o malaking pagdiriwang ang kanilang dinadaluhan.

Sa oras ng pamamahinga ay pinatutugtog niya ang mga lumang plaka na galing sa Pilipinas. Nababalot ang bahay sa magiliw na himig ng awitin ni Conching Rosal, gaya ng "Ang Maya", at iba pang mga kundiman. At bagama't tahimik ang mag-asawa sa pakikinig, ay tila musika ang naglalapat ng salita sa kanilang mga tikom na labi na nagpapahayag ng walang maliw na paggalang, pag-aalaga at pagmamahal sa isa't isa.

Sa hindi inaasahang pangyayari, isang umaga, ay di na nagising sa pagtulog ang butihing maybahay. Biglang dumilim at gumuho ang magandang daigdig na ginagalawan ni Felizardo.

Dumanas siya ng matindi at mahabang pagluluksa at pangungulila. Nawalan na siya ng pakiramdam at pagnanasa sa buhay. Ayaw na niyang makipag-usap sa kanino man. Minsan ay nagkulong siya sa kusina at iniwang sumisingaw ang gaas mula sa kalan. Ibig na niyang magpakamatay. Umalingawngaw ang *fire alarm* sa bahay, sumaklolo ang kapitbahay at dumating ang bombero at *paramedic*; at nakaligtas na naman sa kamatayan ang walang-kamatayang nilalang.

Di naglaon at nagpasiya ang gobyerno, at walang nagawa kundi tumupad sa utos ang kaisa-isang anak ni Felizardo, na noon ay may sarili nang pamilya, na ipagbili na ang bahay at ilagak ang lalaking ulian sa isang *retirement home.*

Mahaba, makasaysayan at lipos ng pakikibaka, kabayanihan at pananabik, kapahamakan at tagumpay ang landas na tinahak ni Felizardo, na nagsimula pa sa Tundo, Maynila at tila magwawakas sa Los Angeles , California , U.S.A.

Umuukilkil sa isip ni Felizardo ang isang naisin: Ang buhay at ang mabuhay ay kabanal-banalang handog ng Diyos sa isang nilalang; nguni't, ang pagbawi sa buhay na iyan, sa pamamagitan din ng kamay ng Diyos, ay isa ring walang kapantay na kabanal-banalang pagbibigay.

3

Old Man of the Mound

Percival Campoamor Cruz

Where did the elves (duwende) and the old men of the mound (nuno sa punso) come from? Were they creatures made by God akin to men? Were men and the creatures of the underground made at the same time? Were men made as small creatures and they got bigger in time? Or were the duwendes and the nunos big in size at the beginning and they got smaller? Why were there duwendes and nunos in the world? Perplexing questions that could explain the mysteries of the universe if only they coud be answered.

Elves were young tiny creatures the size of the human hand. Old men of the mound were older elves just as the name implied. Both lived under the ground. Their living places were marked by mounds – thus the term old men of the mound (nuno sa punso).

If you asked a scholar, he would tell you that the mound was actually soil that kicked up from the diggings of ants and termites. But if you asked a Filipino, educated or not, the mound was the dwelling of the little ones. The mound was an object of reverence.

The male nuno wore long, white beards. While elves were playful, the nuno had a serious disposition and could be easily upset. They could make themselves visible to children, particularly after 6 at night and during the day, between noon and 3. Parents forbade their children from playing in the backyard at these hours.

The inhabitants of the mound got very upset when the mound was stepped on or ran over. They became even more upset when irreverent persons intentionally spat or pissed at the mound.

The little creatures protected their home by spitting in return and when the spit hit a person , that person became sick. The punishment was quite equitable. Kick the mound and the foot became swollen. Spit at the mound and the mouth became sore. Piss at the mound and there would be a urinary problem. Ordinary doctors could not treat the maladies brought about by the duwende or the nuno. Only arbularyos or faith healers could apply a remedy.

One of the remedies was to bring food and wine to the mound coupled with an apology.

For a reason nobody knew, the nuno was attracted to fat females, humans or animals alike.

Humans learned from experience. When they walked across a place that they suspected there were mounds belonging to the duwende and the nuno, they asked for permission to pass – "Tabi, tabi po, apo" – which means, "Please move aside, old man; may I have permission to pass".

Life in the underground, more or less, replicated life above the ground. The duwendes and the nunos worked using ants and termites as their beasts of burden. The women sewed clothes and cooked. The men gathered foods and woods for the fireplace. They were good carpenters and mechanics. They built houses and furniture, they built small motors and gadgets. The community or colony knew how to enjoy. They had feasts and traditions, holidays and sports, dancing and music, social drinking and mirth.

Lately, Bakol always wore an unhappy face. By the way, nunos lived up to 200 years. Bakol who was 100 years was, therefore, in his middle age. A good number of his kind had been kidnapped. He was feeling bad and angry that one of those kidnapped was his beloved Tale.

Every minute his wish was to go out and find Tale. He did not care where fate would take him.

Tandang Puten, the colony elder, had already spoken to Bakol. Get on with your life was Tandang Puten's advise to the distraught being. And Bakol always said he could not forget Tale and he could not move on.

The colony was celebrating the arrival of Spring. Everyone showed up at the town center in their best colorful clothes to be part of the merriest of all celebrations. Everyone was participating in the dancing and eating and drinking. All of a sudden the roof of the mound broke open and everyone got blinded by the glare of the sky. Then fell a net trap and in a quick moment when the net was pulled up about a thousand duwendes and nunos were caught inside, trapped, kidnapped and taken away.

One eventful night, Bakol decided to walk out of the mound. Outside, he could feel the breeze cool his face and skin, a sensation not felt inside the mound. He could see the full moon above and the moonshine provided light to the surrounding field. Not too far from the mound, he could see a house, the house of Raul.

Raul was a human who became friends to the mound dwellers. He played a lot in the backyard when he was just a toddler and became a playmate to the elves. When he grew up to become a young man, he knew a lot about the duwendes and the nunos. He respected them and treated them like his own family.

Bakol wandered close to the house of Raul. He heard Raul talking to someone on the phone and he heard that he was leaving soon for China.

"I will handle the situation, Sir. I'll make sure they cooperate. In the meantime, have patience. Keep the colony well-fed and healthy. . ."

Bakol's hair stood on end. He heard Raul mention "the colony". He kept his ears close to the wall and listened to the rest of the conversation. In the end, he knew what was going on. Raul betrayed the colony. Raul was going to leave for China, where Bakol's kind was taken. He would ascertain that the colony would cooperate in the accomplishment of a mission.

Bakol made his decision. He would keep an eye on Raul. When he left for China, he would go along with him. He would hide himself inside Raul's suitcase. Wherever Raul was going, Bakol knew that he was going, too, to find Tale.

And the trip to China came about.

China had become a world power. Out of the city of Xichang also known as Base 27, China had sent a number of manned space missions into space and to the moon. Now it was time to send a mission to Mars. Chinese taikonauts manned the earlier missions. This time China was sending a colony of little beings to Mars. The idea was to send a one-way mission and begin to populate Mars.

The smaller the spacecraft, the smaller the passengers, the cheaper and more efficient the mission would be. To use the least amount of space and possible fuel when traveling to Mars and yet load all the food, water, oxygen and equipment needed to work the mission and sustain life at the destination planet, smallness was a prerequisite. According to Fraser Cain, a science writer, the spacecraft followed what was called the Hohmann Transfer Orbits. These were curved paths that took advantage of the orbital velocity of planets in order to reach the destination.

When traveling to Mars, a spaceship already had the orbital velocity of going around the Earth. It then fired its rockets to put it onto a transfer orbit with the final destination of Mars. Once it reached Mars, it either fired its rockets again, or used a process called aerobraking to use the Martian atmosphere to slow it down. Earth and Mars had to be at the right positions in their orbits for this method to work, and the launch window only came around once every 25 months. This method used a relatively small amount of fuel. How long did it take to get to Mars using this method? About 214 days.

Getting to Mars was becoming overly important because the earth's resources were dwindling and the living conditions caused by nuclear radiation and environmental pollution were getting worse. Mars was the future. The source of energy and materials. The future home of men should the earth vanish or become inhabitable.

But why send the duwendes and the nunos from the Philippines? And why send them against their will?

Unfortunately, these creatures of the subsoil had no rights. Space missions had experimented with monkeys, dogs, mice, reptiles, insects – they had all been sent out on missions to space and beyond. Many of them never came back. The creatures of the subsoil had freedom and rights no better than those of the animals.

At the opportune time, Bakol showed himself to Raul. And Raul immediately sent him to the colony.

Bakol's fellows were in a frenzy when they saw him. They saw in him a hope. They knew that Bakol was strong and intelligent. They could be saved. And after so many weeks of separation and anxiety, Bakol and Tale got reunited at last.

Bakol spent a lot of time to earn the confidence of the duwendes and nunos. He took the trouble of explaining to them how noble the mission was no matter that the execution was bad. He told them about the opportunities. The high possibility that the place they were being flown to could be a better place than the place they came from. "The important thing is that we are all together in this. We live or die together," Bakol put it in one succinct statement.

At last, Bakol's kind reached out an agreement. Yes, they would cooperate and go along with the mission.

"We have only one condition," Bakol told Raul and Raul's masters, "pull out the ones who are alone, send them back to their homes to be with their loved ones again. As to the rest of us who are with our loved ones now, we will all go."

Since all the kinks have been ironed out and the mission

now had the consent of the mininauts, China went public and announced the first "manned" mission to Mars. Aboard the Chinese spacecraft named "Nuno 1" were 500 duwendes and nunos, males and females, from Pundaquit, Zambales in the Philippines.

When the mission took off, there was a television coverage, and the whole world saw the Chinese and Philippine flags emblazoned on the skin of the spacecraft.

Bakol whispered to Tale as soon as the spacecraft got aloft, "Tale, we will be the Adam and Eve of our generation. I'm really proud we are."

4

Walang Kamag-anak sa Pag-ibig

Percival Campoamor Cruz

Natatandaan ko si Kaka Mundo. Panganay na kapatid siya ng nanay ko. Ang Lola Cion ko ay nakapag-asawa nang makalawa, mangyari ay namatay ang unang asawa. Si Kaka Mundo ay unang anak sa unang asawa at ang nanay ko ay bunsong anak sa pangalawa.

Bata pa ako noon. Sa tuwing pista sa Tundo ay pumupunta kami sa bahay ni Kaka Mundo. Kaugalian noon sa Tundo na kung pista, kaarawan ng Santo Ninyo, ang lahat ng bahay ay may handa. Kilala man o hindi, ang mga dumadayo ay tinatanggap sa kanino mang bahay upang makakain ng masarap.

May sinasabi sa buhay si Kaka Mundo. Mekaniko siya ng sasakyan. Mahusay pa siya sa negosyo. Si Kaka Mundo, nakita ko, ay hari ng mga *jeepney drivers* noong araw. Siya ang may-ari ng humigit-kumulang na limampung *jeepney* na paroo't- parito sa pagitan ng Gagalangin at San Nicolas, sa Tundo.

Maliliit pa ang mga *jeepney* noon, nagsasakay lamang ng siyam, kasama na ang tsuper; ngayon ay malalaki at mahahaba na ang mga *jeepney* – nagsasakay ng mga dalawampu't pitong katao, kasama na ang tsuper. Ang plaka ng maliliit na *jeepney* ay may titik na AC, ibig sabihin ay *"Auto-Calesa"*.

Upang makilala ang mga *jeepney* ni Kaka Mundo, ginawa niyang berde ang kulay ng lahat ng *jeepney* na pag-aari niya.

Sa pook na pinaghihintayan ng *jeepney* ay karaniwang mayroong "kristo". Siya ang tumatawag sa pansin ng mga sasakay at nagbabalita kung saan patungo ang *jeepney*. Binabayaran siya ng tsuper ng kung ilang peseta kapag napuno na ng sakay ang *jeepney*.

Tundo noon ang tirahan ng mga may sinasabi sa Maynila. Di pa sikat noon ang Quezon City at Makati. Nasa Tundo ang mga kalakal at ang *pier* ng mga bapor na papunta sa Bisaya at sa Amerika. Nasa Tundo rin ang Divisoria, ang pinakamalaking pamilihan ng lahat ng pangangailangan. May kasabihan noon, kung ano man ang hinahanap mo ay sa Divisoria mo matatagpuan.

Kung saan pumaparada ang mga *jeepney* sa gabi ay doon din naroroon ang talyer ni Kaka Mundo. Siya mismo ang nangangasiwa sa pag-aayos sa mga *jeepney* kung ang mga ito ay nasisira, doon sa talyer na iyon.

Nang bata pa ako, sa tuwing bibisita kami sa aking Kaka Mundo, ay kailangang magmamano ako sa kanya, bilang tanda ng pagbati at paggalang sa matanda. . . kahit na nangingitim sa dumi at puno ng langis ang kanyang kamay. Nasisilip ko sa isang silid ng talyer na nagbibilang ng pera na iniintrega ng mga tsuper ang asawa ni Kaka Mundo, kasama ang isang katulong. Noong panahong iyon ay papel ang pera, hindi metal. Pagkabilang ng pera ay pinaplantsa nila, gamit ang plantsang pangtuwid sa lukot na damit, ang dagsa-dagsang singko sentimos, diyes sentimos, beinte sentimos – mga perang papel na may iba't ibang kulay.

Mayroong diyes sentimo na metal na napakaliit at karaniwang itinatago ng mga tao sa taynga, sa halip na ilagay sa bulsa. Nagugunita ko ang istorya ng isang napaka-*sexy* na babae na sumakay sa *jeepney*. Maikli ang palda at ang suot na blusa ay talaga namang nakatatawag pansin dahil kita ang lusog ng kanyang mga bundok. Nang bababa na ay nagsabi ng, "Para na, mama. Sa tabi l'ang." Sabay dukot ng diyes sentimos na nasa kanyang kanang taynga.

Ang pasahe noon ay diyes sentimos. Kaya nga may palaala sa loob ng jeepney na nagsasabi ng: "Upong diyes po lamang". Pakiusap ito sa mga babae na kung umupo ay patagilid, tuloy ay wala nang espasyong maupuan ang bagong kasasakay na pasahero. Isa pang paboritong paalaala na mababasa sa loob ng *jeepney* ay: "God knows hudas not pay."

May anak na lalaki si Kaka Mundo; si Eddie, Kuya Eddie ang tawag ko. Wala siyang hilig na mag-aral. Natural na ang kinahantungan niya ay ang pagiging mekaniko at katulong ng tatay niya sa talyer at sa pagpapatakbo ng mga *jeepney*. Samantalang ang isa pang anak na lalaki, si

Dengdeng, ay naging abogado at kumandidato pa sa pagiging konsehal sa Tundo. Nagkaroon si Dengdeng ng mga kabayong pangkarera na inilalaban sa mga hipodromo ng San Lazaro at Santa Ana.

Hindi nabuhay nang matagal ang asawa ni Kaka Mundo. Palibhasa ay may katabaan, siya ay nagkaroon ng sakit sa puso; at nang lumaon ay iyon ang kanyang ikinamatay. Malaking babae at malapad si Kakang Goneng. Nagpagawa pa ng kabaong na espesyal para sa kanya dahil di siya husto sa karaniwang kabaong. Nalungkot sa pag-iisa si Kaka Mundo. Nawala ang gana niya sa pagtatrabaho at napabayaan ang negosyo.

Nasa kamay ni Kuya Eddie ang ikalulunas ng kalungkutan ng kanyang ama. Isinasama niya ang ama sa kanyang mga lakad. Nakilala ni Kaka Mundo ang kasintahan ni Kuya Eddie na ang pangalan ay Lumeng. Maputi si Lumeng at maamo ang mukha. Maikli ang buhok kahi't na noong mga panahon na iyon ay mahabang buhok ang uso. Masasabing si Lumeng ay babaeng makabago.

May mga panahon na si Lumeng ay bumibisita sa bahay nina Kaka Mundo at Kuya Eddie. Tumutulong siya sa mga gawaing bahay. Nagluluto at nagbabantay kay Kaka Mundo, tila nars na tagabigay ng gamot at inumin ng matanda.

Kahi't anong alaga at pang-aliw ang subukan nina Kuya Eddie at Lumeng ay di nagkakabisa sa aking Kaka Mundo. Palagi siyang malungkot at walang sigla.

Isang araw ay nasabi ni Kuya Eddie, "Tatay, palagay ko ay dapat kayong mag-asawang muli. Bata pa kayo at malakas pa."

"Anak, setenta na ako, paano naman naging bata? Sino pa ang magkakagusto sa akin?" sagot ni Kaka Mundo.

Marami pa ang iibig kay Kaka Mundo. Kahi't na ang mga bata-batang mga babae ay iibig sa kanya. Sapagka't kahi't na siya ay sitenta anyos ay maganda pa ang pangangatawan ni Kaka Mundo. Maskulado siya at malalakas ang mga bisig. Maganda ang tindig at kung lumakad ay mabilis.

Higit sa lahat ay mayaman si Kaka Mundo. May kaya siya sa buhay – may mga *jeepney* na araw-araw ay nag-uuwi ng libong pisong kita sa kanyang bulsa. Malaki ang kanyang bahay at mayroon pang mga paupahang *accessoria*s sa Tundo. Ang iibig kay Kaka Mundo ay tiyak na giginhawa ang buhay.

Dahil sa malimit na pagbisita ni Lumeng at pag-aalaga kay Kaka Mundo ay nagkaroon ng malapit na pagkikilala ang dalawa. Unti-unti ay nagkakaroon ng interes kay Lumeng si Kaka Mundo. Sa tuwing lalapit ang magandang babae upang tulungan siyang makainom ng gamot o di kaya ay ng *refresco* na malamig na tubig o katas ng buko ay nalalanghap niya ang nakahuhumaling na pabango ni Lumeng. "Kung mag-aasawa akong muli ay isang kagaya ni Lumeng ang aking hahanapin. Kung di l'ang sana nagkasundo na si Lumeng at si Eddie. . ." bulong ni Kaka Mundo sa sarili.

"Tatay, lumabas kayo ng bahay. Mamasyal kayo. Ayain ninyo ang inyong mga kaibigan at maglibang kayo," payo ni Eddie.

"Kung alam mo lamang, anak; ang magpapaligaya sa akin ay naririto sa bahay palagi. Hindi na ako kailangang pumunta pa sa malayo. Nguni't papaano ang gagawin ko. May interes ako kay Lumeng, nguni't siya ay kasintahan mo na!" Sabi ni Kaka Mundo sa kanyang sarili lamang.

Isang araw ay hindi na nakapagpigil si Kaka Mundo. Nang tiyak niya na si Eddie ay abala sa pagkukumpini ng *jeepney* at si Lumeng ay lumapit upang ayain siya sa pananghalian. . .

"Mang Mundo, baka gutom na kayo, handa na po ang pananghalian," paanyaya ni Lumeng.

"Lumeng, ang gutom ko ay hindi sa pagkain, kundi sa pagmamahal. Anong gagawin mo kung sabihin kong may pagtingin ako sa iyo?" tanong ni Kaka Mundo.

Namula ang mukha ni Lumeng. Hindi nakapagsalita kaagad bago nagsabi ng, "Mapagbiro kayo Mang Mundo."

Paglipas ng ilang linggo ay nagbalik ang dating sigla ni Kaka Mundo. Nakukuha na niyang sumipol at kung minsan ay umaawit pa habang nagkukumpini ng *jeepney*. Naging masipag siyang muli at mapag-alaala sa kanyang negosyo. Napansin ni Eddie ang malaking pagbabago sa kilos at kalagyan ng pag-iisip ng ama.

Paano ay pumayag ang babaeng nakursunadahan niya na sila ay lumabas at mag-aliw. Ilang gabing sunud-sunod na sila ay nagpupunta sa pasyalan – sa Luneta o di kaya ay sa tabing-dagat. Kumakain sa *restaurant.* Nagsasayaw sa *night club.*

Pagkatapos ay nakahahanap sila ng pag-iisa sa silid ng isang *motel* at doon ay nagkakaroon ng katuparan ang pagsisilakbo ng kanilang mga damdamin.

Maligaya na si Kaka Mundo nguni't sa kabilang dako ay binabagabag siya ng kanyang konsyensya. Sabi niya sa sarili, "Kaawa-awa naman si Eddie. Paano ko kaya sasabihin sa kanya ang nangyayari? Naging Hudas ako sa sarili kong anak!"

Isang araw ay nag-usap ang mag-ama. Sabi ni Kuya Eddie, "Tatay, nagpasiya kami ni Lumeng na magpakasal na. Nagpasiya kami na magpakasal sa susunod na buwan."

Muntik nang ibuga ni Kaka Mundo ang kahihigop na kape. "Magpapakasal kayo ni Lumeng!? Anak, hindi mo alam ang iyong ginagawa."

"Bakit, Tatay, kapuwa kami may edad na ni Lumeng. Tiyak na alam namin ang aming ginagawa." Sagot ni Kuya Eddie.

"Ang ibig kong sabihin ay . . ." at ipinagtapat ng ama sa anak ang mga nangyari.

"Patawarin mo ako, Eddie. Ako ang minamahal ni Lumeng at ang pagpayag niya na makipagkasal sa iyo ay wala sa kanyang loob."

"Kung gayon ay kayo ang magpakasal sa kanya sa susunod na buwan. Handa ba kayo?" tila hamon na ibinato ni Kuya Eddie sa kanyang tatay.

Sa araw na pinagkasunduan ay nagkaroon ng malaking kasalan sa katedral ng Santo Ninyo sa Tundo.

Sabay ikinasal ang mag-amang Kaka Mundo at Kuya Eddie ko.

Si Kuya Eddie kay Lumeng na kanyang matagal nang kasintahan.

Si Kaka Mundo kay Loleng, ang kakambal ni Lumeng, na siyang naging nars niya at kapareha sa sayawan at sa pugad ng pag-ibig.

Binalak nina Kuya Eddie at Lumeng ang lahat. At ang pakana ay nagbunga ng maganda.

5

Congo and the Philippines

Allen Gaborro

(Allen Gaborro is a resident book reviewer for the San Francisco-based Philippine News weekly. Allen has composed articles on historical, cultural, and political issues. Allen also has a bi-monthly column in the San Francisco-based FilAm Star newspaper. He is also working as a contributing international affairs writer for an English-language publication in Japan, as well as on a manuscript for a novel. He just published his The Gaborro Reader, available at www.amazon.com in paperback and kindle edition.)

Dateline, Feb 7, 2011
Published in Ambassadeur Magazine

The current generation of what the late Tony Judt wrote as one that was "obsessed with the pursuit of material wealth" was also guilty of being "indifferent to so much else," the study of history being near the top of that "so much else" list. History, to put it another way, has become subjected to ennui by a modern civilization that apparently has better things to look forward to. But history is still dynamic and appealing to those of us who are not ready to put the final touches on historical studies. Contrary to what many people in Western(ized) societies believe, the attempt to restore history as a wealth of inadequately-explored or politically-repressed events and personalities should not be made out to be some prosaic diversion that pointlessly brings us back to an extraneous past.

Given the world's present troubles, history as a pertinent topic has to work hard to make itself visible through the morass of a modernity that many are convinced has gotten out of control. But to ignore history is to, to paraphrase the famous Santayana line, to reprise the mistakes it is laden with. Being so contemptuous of history is also to compound those mistakes, thereby leading us to base how Western civilization is structured and programmed on what is an expediently distorted picture of historical reality.

Keeping those ruminations in mind, there are two historical events that I would like to touch on here, events that have receded in the Western historical consciousness, not that either of them ever really shimmered in the light of mainstream historiographical narratives. The first one is the story of Belgium's colonial enterprise in the African Congo under King Leopold II, beginning in 1885 and ending in 1908. The second transports us back to America's imperial campaign to forcibly subdue the Philippine Islands at the turn of the century. That endeavor, officially lasting from 1899 to 1903 (but actually dragging on in a war of attrition for another 11 years), was every bit as violent and bloody as Belgium's imperial project in Africa.

It was with a systematic combination of corruption, political spin, Machiavellian maneuvering, and a readiness to resort to what amounted to barbarism, that King Leopold II of Belgium sought to turn the Congo, a huge territory that was about seventy times larger than Belgium itself, into literally his own private property.

For official reasons related to ostensibly-benevolent causes and so that diminutive Belgium would gain respect on the world stage, Leopold secured Belgian control over the Congo in the 1884 Conference of Berlin which divided Africa among the European colonial powers. However, Leopold's ulterior motive for colonizing the Congo morally lagged behind his stated purposes. His real motive was to exploit the territory's vast natural resources for his personal aggrandizement. Leopold accomplished this beyond his wildest dreams.

Leopold accumulated a massive amount of riches from Belgium's Congo investment. Ivory, rubber, and other minerals were the source of his incredible fortune. But it is the means of that fortune that made him in the view of author Adam Hochschild, a brazen profiteer, a colossal megalomaniac, an enslaver of men, women, and children, and worst of all, a mass murderer. Hochschild's best selling 1998 book, "King Leopold Ghost," chronicles the history of Leopold's brutal subjugation of the Congolese people.

According to Hochschild and other independent histories of the Congo Free State as it was called under Leopold's rule, as many as 10 million Congolese died as a result of his majesty's incomparable greed. Under Leopold's aegis, rubber and ivory quotas were imposed on Congolese slave laborers. Failure to reach the quotas were met with beatings, rapes, the hacking off of the hands of men, women, and children alike, and with killings on a wide scale. As horrible as it is, the story of Leopold's Congolese nightmare is worth reading about for its relevance to the modern-day massacres in Rwanda and in Sudan's Darfur region.

For decades, the United States has tried to project itself around the globe as a paragon of freedom, human rights, and democracy. As much as anywhere else, this shining image was badly tarnished in the turn of the century Philippines, a land that then US President William McKinley maintained had to be colonized "for humanity's sake."

Influenced by a conjunction of economic, geopolitical, religious, and racial rationalizations, America, at the time a rising industrial power, saw great dividends from colonizing the Philippines just as the archipelago was ending centuries of repressive Spanish colonial rule. The McKinley administration would defend the takeover of the Philippines by helping remove the tyranny of Spanish colonialism and by promising to institute democratic institutions and values in the islands. In other words, the US as a colonial master wanted to "civilize" the Filipinos, otherwise designated as America's "little brown brothers."

However, Filipinos had burgeoning notions of independence in their heads, thus confounding Washington's imperial ambitions, albeit for the interim. So when the US deployed soldiers in the islands in the last stages of Spain's defeat at the hands of anti-colonial Filipino fighters, it was only a matter of time that tensions between American and Filipino forces boiled over into a live conflict. What resulted was the Philippine-American War, a conflagration that bore historical witness to imperialistic ruthlessness and savagery.

During the Philippine-American War, the United States had to combat outgunned but determined Filipino fighters. Doing so would cost the lives of about 4,000 American soldiers. The fighting would also kill anywhere from 250,000 to 1,000,000 Filipinos. Many of the Filipino deaths resulted from the Americans' application of torture, scorched-earth programs, and operation of concentration camps. Several civilian massacres at the hands of American soldiers added dramatically to the death toll. One such prominent massacre took place in the town of Balangiga in 1901. It was there that US General Jacob H. Smith gave the order to shoot any Filipino male over the age of ten because they were in his view, capable of utilizing weapons.

A most hopeful note concerning the tragic episodes in the Congo and in the Philippines is that the passage of time has engendered an honest and rational reflection on the historical depravities committed by Western nations against non-Western ones. What is distressing about this is that it has taken so long for Western societies to collectively recognize and acknowledge what are incredulous truths about their past. My particular dismay lies in that people continue to pass over what are by now, substantiated historical conclusions, conclusions that they generally assume to be too distant to be of any didactic value today.

6

Divorce In the Philippines

Allen Gaborro

Dateline, June 24, 2011
Published in FILAM STAR

I'm glad to say that I read and hear about a generation of youthful and middle-aged Filipinos who are well on their way to becoming visionary, tech-savvy, and socio-politically progressive citizens of the 21st century. What is endearing about these Filipinos is that they loathe the long-standing, retrograde attitudes and practices that many from the older generations before them have put up with or offered trite rationalizations for.

On behalf of these dynamic, enlightened, and precocious Filipinos, I would like to assert that Philippine society stands to gain from the surfeit of reservations they have on the Philippine Roman Catholic Church's archaic socio-political positions. I also want to express my unstinting support of the proposed legislation to make divorce legal in the Philippines, something that has been a long time in coming. What the Philippines has had for decades is a farcical adaptation of the "annulment" concept which is really a purgatorial template for failed marital relations. What I mean to say is that "annulment" is supposed to lie somewhere between an actual divorce and the living institution of marriage.

Listening to the Philippine Catholic Church defend

its disapproval of divorce is like listening to the Republicans blame Barack Obama for the declining American economy. The Church likes to point out that by prohibiting legalized divorce families will remain intact. Short on facts and even less on understanding, the Church's stance does not make the grade in fulfilling the expectations of a society that is struggling to make itself relevant in a globalized, information-saturated world.

In our exacting, supra-technological ethos, the Church's reiteration of grandiose criticisms leveled at the divorce legislation is something to behold. While thousands in the Philippines are addressing their everyday temporal survival, the Catholic Church instead harps on the contradiction between artificial birth control programs and God's presumed will on human reproduction, and on the supposedly perilous impact of legalized divorce on the sacrosanct conception of the family unit.

In short, rather than robustly promote anti-poverty campaigns or essential population control strategies or tap into its massive reservoir of financial assets and reserves to help the disadvantaged, the Roman Catholic Church of the Philippines hides behind a wall of religious intransigence and churns out opinions and positions on society that have no place in the new millennium. Coming from the low end of the nation's sociological and demographical priorities, the Church and its elitist, bishopric leadership will not be satisfied until both the reproductive health and divorce bills are torn asunder, to use religious language. For the Church hierarchy, the perpetuation of their religious ideology has always come first before the welfare of the people.

Today, you can walk down many streets in the

Philippines and find a majority of people who favor legalized divorce. It is against this popular grain that the Philippine Catholic Church stands. What its leaders forget is that sometimes marriages don't work out for a variety of reasons. It's sad, but that just the way of the world between some husbands and wives. The Church cannot change that by forcing couples to stay together as a spiritually-certified formality, rather than as a loving union.

Not all husbands are saints and not all wives are angels. That obvious statement validates the need for at least a separation for the good of the two parties in a dysfunctional marriage. If the separation is on a trial basis, that is one thing. But if it becomes permanent, then it is all but divorce in name. Isn't it inconsistent to be opposed to "divorce" but at the same time to allow it when it's a "separation"?

Everyone knows that married couples separate all the time in the Philippines. Many of them end up living apart for good and find other life-partners. It is outlandish to prompt people to believe that this is, when it comes down to it, somehow not the same thing as divorcing. But this absurdity is what the Catholic Church pitches to its faithful.

Besides, if the idea of the unity of family is under distress in the Philippines, I would blame it more on here-and-now concerns than on a breakdown of spiritual values which would be more of the symptom than the cause. The Church therefore, should stop its ranting and raving and join the rest of the Roman Catholic global community—
with the exception of the Vatican of course—in finally legalizing divorce.

7

RH Production Bill

Allen Gaborro

Dateline, May 27, 2011
Published in FILAM STAR

It is said that life is fleeting enough for someone who manages to live well into adulthood and old age. How about for the humanoid entity (if we can use this term) that is created at the moment of conception? In that entity, or "being" if you prefer, throbs the possibility and potential of human life. But can it really be considered alive at that instance? Can it be considered a person, a living human being, a mortal individual? The Catholic Church, as it is steered by Vatican doctrine, says yes, that the moment of conception is the indisputably sacred and irrevocable genesis of human life.

There is a seismic convergence of forces that forms the other side of the divide of this argument. These forces, among others, are the modern ethos, scientific thought, activist feminism, the rights of the individual in a secular society, and the principle of a female's autonomy over her own body.

Added to this whole array of dissenting discourses is the democratic concept of the separation of church and state. Right now, this concept is being confronted by the Roman Catholic Church of the Philippines which has expressed its wholehearted opposition to the proposed

Reproductive Health Bill. A basic argument of the Church against the bill is that it promotes artificial contraception, a key component of the pending legislation.

Contraception to the Church is tantamount to committing a form of evil. One such form is based on the belief that it is akin to murder in the eyes of God. Now I strongly disagree with this, but I wish to avoid conducting an intractable debate that is attributed to an interpretation founded on religious faith and another that is tied to a more profane worldview. What concerns me more in regards to the uproar over the Reproductive Health bill is that it has been triggered by the Philippine Roman Catholic Church's hardcore and dogmatic Christianization of what is at the center of it, a public health, welfare, and demographics issue.

As I have written in the past, the Church, as much as anyone else, is entitled to its opinion on reproductive health. The Philippines is a free country after all (at least on the surface) and constructive disagreement can be a good thing. The problem begins however, when the Church uses fear, intimidation, coercion, unmerited criticism, and what is the declining weight of its socio-political authority to influence public policy, a field that is outside of their core metaphysical jurisdiction. The Philippine Catholic Church, as it is guided by the self-referential and self-righteous club that is called the Catholic Bishops' Conference of the Philippines (CBCP), has all but exceeded the moral, legal, institutional, and political boundaries of the separation of church and state.

From unilaterally breaking off discussions with the government, to contemplating legal action, to seriously advocating civil disobedience, and finally, to having some of its august members label President Noynoy Aquino as anti-Christian and bring up the issue of his possible excommunication, the CBCP has bared its zeal in blurring the crucial line between pragmatic public policy and private, otherworldly morality.

The concept of the separation of church and state in the Philippines will invariably be broken if the Catholic Church has its way in the RH bill battle. This would suit the church hierarchy just fine except that it would represent a dangerous lack of understanding of the socio-economic and demographic realities of modern Philippine existence and of the sexual drives that are naturally inherent in every human being. But because of a refusal to put any store in timely perspectives that might nevertheless be deemed by hypersensitive religious absolutists as seditious to the Church's teachings, any real reconciliation between the demands of modern society, the inner and physical struggle of the contemporary human condition, and the sacrosanct values of Roman Catholicism, is nothing more than a remote prospect.

If only the Philippine Catholic Church would accept its proper place in a democratic society and focus on piously ministering to its flock, which is its main occupation in the first place. Better yet, if only the stubborn Church prelates would recognize that many present-day Filipino Catholics are not the meek worshippers that they once were and that significant numbers of them actually support the RH bill.

8

Take the Amazing "Wow! Kay Ganda ng Pilipinas" Challenge

Peter Allan Mariano

(Peter Allan Mariano is an electronics manufacturing engineer, writer, broadcaster, web designer and entrepreneur. He has written for several international websites and online publications through his internet marketing company Linsk2prosperity and is currently the Editor-in-Chief of Health Connections magazine and a columnist for the newspaper-magazine Tuwid. He is the website administrator, content editor and feature reporter for the radio program Talakayan at Kalusugan @ DWBL1242. He is the moderator of the entrepreneurial society Entreplink Philippines and is the officer-in-charge of The Big NM – Network Management for Filipinos)

Dateline, Jun 2011
First published in www.bestphilippineattractions.com

The recent brouhaha involving the "Pilipinas Kay Ganda"

campaign by the Department of Tourism (DoT) brought the online world into an uproar, many pointing accusing fingers at the people behind this botched tourism campaign. The DoT bounced back with a new slogan, "Pilipinas, Tara Na!" urging Pinoys to be tourists in their own country, inviting all to visit and explore the myriad festivals, destinations and other Best Philippine Attractions the whole archipelago has to offer.

For whatever campaign slogan the tourism body can come up with: be it "Wow Philippines!" or "Pilipinas Kay Ganda" or a mixed "Wow! Kay Ganda ng Pilipinas" – there's no doubt in everyone's mind, local or foreign, that the Philippines is truly blessed with natural wonders and amazing sights to behold. The sad fact is many Pinoys are simply content on staying in their own abode somewhere in the country, not even realizing how beautiful other parts of the nation can be. Some have travelled abroad and have seen the sights and sounds of nearby Asia or faraway Europe – without even setting foot on another island in the country they call home.

The challenge now is this: **How Many of the 7100+ Islands Can You Explore?**

The Philippine archipelago is a cluster of 7100+ islands extending for nearly 2000 kilometers across the warm tropical waters of the Pacific. The country is home to an evolutionary explosion of more than 4000 species of trees, 160 species of mammals and over 240 species of reptiles all packed within this small geographical landscape that Filipinos call home.

Despite the fact of the country's close proximity to our other Asian neighbors, Filipinos are the least "oriental" of them all and has this unique ability to blend well with any culture, race or creed from anywhere in the world and everywhere the Filipino Diaspora has reached. And yet, Filipinos still maintain all the enigmatic qualities that are truly Pinoy... qualities that are unique and found only in the Philippines.

And that is what the symbol above signifies... the Philippine archipelago symbolized by a single island... a single mass of land that can be called truly our own.

For indeed the Philippines is ONE.

Despite the many pockets of land sprawled across the Philippines seas.... despite the small intricacies and peculiarities each inhabitant has... despite the differences in dialects and unique customs.... the Philippines and the Filipino is still ONE – one loving heart, one friendly disposition, one dream and one hope for the nation.

And if you come to know the language, you will surely

exclaim..... **Wow!... Kay Ganda ng Pilipinas!** (*Wow! How Beautiful is the Philippines!*)

This is a call for challenge... to Filipinos, non-Filipinos, and Filipinos-at-heart... to come and explore each of the 7,100+ islands and know firsthand what makes every island tick.... what makes every island beautiful... what makes every inhabitant truly Filipino.... what makes us ONE.

It may seem like an impossible task... if given all the resources and allowed to travel to one Philippine destination every month for the rest of your life. But wouldn't that be one very exciting and very worthwhile impossibility? Wow!

The race is on.... now!

9

Your Thoughts

MLMunoz

Thoughts, albeit intangible, are not inanimate. They are vibrating energies with electromagnetic properties that affect your whole bodily function—and radiate outward to create your environment. Each thought has its own vibrational frequency, according to what you're thinking, and the intensity of what the thoughts make you feel. For instance, if your predominant thoughts are negative, you attract negative circumstances—and people. "What you sow is what you reap," so the Bible says. We, of course, take this to mean that when we do something good we must be rewarded with something of equal value, or possibly more. In other words, we refer to our action as the act of "sowing" and the outcome of that action as the "reaping." And when we do not get the equivalent of what we have "sown," we feel cheated, frustrated, confused. "How come my neighbor who doesn't even go to church won the lottery? (The fanatic would say it's the work of the devil.) "How come I pray all the time for God to protect me but I was mugged?" The strong of faith would say, "God is testing me." And the not so strong ones become disillusioned, or doubtful.

Negative thoughts come in many forms. It can be self-pity, self-condemnation, resentment, fear, guilt, worries and a lot of times, beliefs that were handed down from generation to generation.

Back home we have this belief that if you get caught in the rain you must take a shower as soon as you get home, or you will catch a cold. Or that if you are exposed to someone with a contagious virus, you're sure to be next. I was probably too carefree to believe in any of this (The ones I took seriously were, "Blessed are the poor," and "Money is the root of all evil.") because I never felt threatened by the rain. The rain evokes in me a feeling of wonder—and pleasure. I remember when I was in high-school, I'd fold my umbrella when I'm halfway home, then tilt my head back so the rain would fall on my face—and when no one is looking, I'd stick out my tongue and taste it. When I get home, I don't rush to the bathroom to take a shower. I simply wipe my hair and change into dry clothes. To this day, I never get a cold from the rain or get contaminated by someone with the flu or even the dreaded sore eyes.

In other words, "sowing" starts from our thoughts (after all, our actions are not always in harmony with our thoughts) as in "What you think you become" or "What you expect you get." So let's go back to the neighbor who never goes to church but won the lottery. Surely it's not that the secret to winning is not going to church. Maybe it had something to do with his thoughts and beliefs? Maybe he has a prosperity consciousness, has no habit of feeling sorry for himself and does not believe that money is the root of all evil. Above all, maybe he does not feel guilty about having money—therefore he doesn't believe that if he becomes rich something tragic will happen to him.

All of us wants to be rich—but for some, there is this deep-seated fear that we may not even be consciously aware of; that we have to give up something in exchange for it (like health, loss of a loved one, etc.) so we unconsciously block wealth from our lives.

What about the person who keeps praying for protection and does not get it? It is because the very act of asking for protection reflects the fear that you feel—and fear is a negative emotion. While the thoughts of muggers and rapists run through your mind, you emit negative vibrations that attract like effects.

Ironically, it's not what we want that occupy our thoughts but what we are afraid of. Like, we all want to be safe at home, and to ensure this safety we secure our doors with 3 giant padlocks and hide the kitchen knife under the bed—for a possible encounter with an intruder. Why, isn't this almost like expecting someone to break into our house?

So next time, be careful. Not of muggers and rapists but of YOUR THOUGHTS.

10

Common Money-Mistakes OFWs Make

Alvin T. Tabanag, RFP

About the author
Founder and Chief-Trainer
PINOY SMART SAVERS LEARNING CENTER
(Intl. Best Provider of Employee Financial Education)
"Helping ordinary Filipinos achieve financial freedom!"
http://www.pinoysmartsavers.com
http://www.facebook.com/alvin.tabanag
Tel.No.: +63 46 416-1385, +63 917 502-3149

Update: June 28, 2011

The BSP's second quarter Consumer Expectations Survey for 2011 showed that the number of OFW households that set aside money for savings has grown to 44 percent – a very substantial increase from the 7.2 percent in 2007. However, since there are an estimated 8.7 to 11 million overseas Filipinos, we are still looking at millions of OFWs who don't save at all. This is very unfortunate because most OFWs have the capacity to accumulate adequate savings which can help them secure their families' financial future. It's really sad that many OFWs are still unable to significantly raise their families' standard of living even after years of working abroad.

I believe one of the main reasons why a lot of OFW families continue to suffer from financial distress is improper money management. Although in some cases an OFW's financial troubles may have been due to circumstances beyond his control (e.g. foreign employers not paying them, victimized by illegal recruiters, displacement due to "Saudization" of jobs, etc.), I'm convinced that most money problems confronting OFWs are due to financial missteps they've committed time and again.

Here are some common money-mistakes that OFWs (and millions of other Pinoys in the country) make and what they can do about it.

1. Reckless spending. My kumpare who worked in the Middle East for several years had this to say about OFWs and their money: *"karamihan sa OFW nagugulat sa perang nahahawakan nila kumpara sa kinikita sa Pinas."* The sudden and enormous jump in income also brings a feeling of empowerment. The OFW now feels he has the power to purchase the things that he and his family have wanted for so long. And so he begins to buy stuff that bring instant gratification like furniture, appliances, computers and electronic gadgets. The family begins to engage in more leisure activities like eating out and going on vacation because they can now afford it. There is nothing wrong with this as long as you keep it under control.

Unrestrained spending, especially on things that you don't really need, can lead to financial ruin. Do not spend as if money will not stop flowing. Overseas work is supposed to be temporary. Sooner or later OFWs will return home and the big income they've been accustomed to will stop coming in. What happens then if you've spent most your money on unnecessary things? Just because you're earning big doesn't mean you have to become a big spender and start living a luxurious lifestyle. Exercise discipline in spending your money. Do not let your expenses catch up with your income, otherwise the money you've worked so hard for will go nowhere. Even if you can afford it, do not spend too much on items you can live without because these will not help you secure your future.

2. Lack of long-term financial goals. Many OFWs and their families spend recklessly because they don't have any long-term goals. What's important to them is to enjoy life to the max now. Their attitude is to live for today and forget about the future. Well, the future will not take care of itself. You should give equal, if not, more importance to your family's future and start preparing for it now! Set and prioritize goals that really matter. Having a 100-inch LCD HDTV in your bedroom is not a very smart goal. Before you buy your kids expensive gadgets ask yourself first if you have already secured their college education. Among the important financial goals that you can make besides securing your children's education are accumulating savings for your retirement, setting aside money for your own house and putting up capital for your own business. Whenever you intend to spend money think about your goals and ask yourself if the expense will bring you closer your goal or farther from it.

3. Not saving consistently & not saving enough. The first thing that comes to mind when people start earning a bigger income is how they will spend the money. The first thing that you should be excited about is how much more you can save now with a higher income. When you receive your salary your top priority is to set aside a substantial amount for your savings and live off on what remains.

Make it a habit to save regularly. Saving should not be an "on and off" activity. Set aside every month at least 20 percent of your income. Save more if you can. Many OFWs have the capacity to save 30 to 50 percent (perhaps even more) of their income. Try to save as much as you can while you are still earning well because it will not last forever. But do not overdo it to the point that your stinginess will already affect your family's comfort and well-being. *Lahat ng sobra ay hindi maganda kahit sa pag-iipon.*

4. *Failing to invest money wisely.* While 44 percent of OFW families save, only a tiny fraction - 5.7 percent - use their funds for investments. You should realize that it's not enough to save. You should invest your money to make it grow bigger and faster which will allow you to reach your financial goals earlier. In fact, you may very well miss your financial targets if you do not invest and grow your money. If you keep your funds in a regular savings account that pays a teeny-weeny interest rate, you will actually lose some purchasing power because your money is not growing as fast as the increase in prices of goods and services. At the very least your money should keep pace with inflation. Your investment options include long-term time deposit accounts (which is not really an investment vehicle but a deposit product but nonetheless a good and safe way to grow your money), treasury bills and bonds, government securities, mutual funds and unit investment trust funds, insurance and pre-need products and real estate. Putting up your own business is also a great way to invest your hard-earned money. Just make sure that you know exactly what you are getting into.

5. *Not teaching family members about responsible money management.* OFWs have to endure prolonged loneliness just to earn more in the hope of improving the quality of life of their loved ones. They work very hard, scrimp and live frugally so that they can remit a bigger amount to their families. Unfortunately, some folks back home squander the money that's sent to them, spending it whenever they feel like it. (Sometimes it is the OFW's fault because he spoils the spouse and kids.)

If your family is wasting a lot of money on non-essential items, you have to put your foot down. Demand that they use responsibly the money you worked hard for. Explain to them that there are things far more important than indulging in stuff that provides instant but short-lived satisfaction. Ask your household to create a reasonable budget for their expenses and have them stick to it. Monitor closely how they spend the money until they learn how to manage it well. I often tell OFWs who bring my book with them abroad to also leave a copy for their family so they will also learn about responsible money management. Every member of the family should do their part if it aspires for a brighter and more secure financial future.

More Money-mistakes by OFWs

By: Alvin T. Tabañag, www.pinoysmartsavers.com

Millions of OFW families continue to suffer from financial stress despite the significant boost in the OFWs' income. Many of these money problems can be traced to mismanagement of their finances. Here are some more money-mistakes that many OFWs make.

1. Sending all your savings to the family. This will not be a problem if your family back home knows how to manage money responsibly. We've all heard of sob stories about a how the spouse in the Philippines wasted the money sent by the OFW and when the OFW returns there's hardly anything to show for his hard work abroad. If your family cannot be trusted with large sums of money, it's best that you don't give them full access to your savings. You can retain control of your funds by opening an account under your name and putting some (or most) of your savings into this account. You can open this personal (or investment) account in the Philippines or in the country where you work. However, I recommend that you keep a Philippine account. Your family may find it difficult to get their hands on your foreign account in case something happens to you. Besides, you will be helping the country more if you keep your money in the Philippines.

2. Not planning for life after OFW work. Most OFWs will eventually return home for good, either by choice or forced to cut short their stint abroad due to unplanned or unexpected events like closure of the company or getting seriously ill. I recently got an email from an OFW who asked about how he can better prepare for retirement. He's coming back permanently in a few years but will still have a job in the Philippines. He's among the lucky ones who have jobs to fall back on after working as an OFW. Many other returning OFWs will be added to the country's unemployment or underemployment statistics and with limited savings, it will just be a matter of time before these ex-OFWs start to suffer from financial problems.

It is crucial then that OFWs prepare for post-OFW life as soon as possible. Planning way ahead of time will make preparation a bit easier and will give you more options. Save as much as you can while still working abroad and invest your savings. If you can't save enough to retire permanently, then you will have to keep on working (as an employee or your own boss) when you come back. Continue enhancing existing skills and learn new ones to improve your chances of landing a job when you return. Develop other sources of income back home (e.g. rental properties and small business) while you're still in foreign soil so that you will have a steady source of funds when you return and stay for good.

3. Taking on too much debt. A large number of OFWs incur debt when they are first deployed. You just have to go near the POEA building in Ortigas to see that OFW loans is big business. Agents of lending companies are always there to distribute flyers with many of their target customers keenly examining the loans they are offering. I can understand OFWs borrowing money to cover expenses for deployment because placement fees today far exceed whatever savings they have. What is troubling is OFWs unnecessarily taking on additional debt because they are now earning more. *"I-charge mo na lang sa credit card yung gusto mong kumikinang na sapatos at glow in the dark na make-up, tutal may pambayad na tayo nyan!"* or *"Sige, kunin mo yung voice-activiated TV na binibenta ng Bombay o umutang ka sa 5-6 para mabili mo yung gusto mong imitation na LV bag!"* is something you might hear from an OFW. If you have to borrow money, do so because it is necessary and important. Do not borrow to support extravagant spending.

4. Accumulating unproductive assets. To a typical OFW, investing means buying tangible items that he can see, touch and feel. Ask him where he has invested his earnings and the usual answer will include any or all of the following: house and lot, appliances, furniture, computers, electronic gadgets, car, motorcycle and jewelry. While some of these are valuable assets, many are not productive, meaning they decrease in value over time and doesn't bring more money into your pocket. In fact, some will make you spend more like fuel, maintenance and insurance for a vehicle. A money-smart OFW will acquire items that will likely increase in value over the years and/or increase his income. Accumulating items that continually decline in value is like slow-burning your money. Besides highly tangible assets like real estate and a car used for business, there are other valuable assets that are less tangible but are great investments nonetheless like investment-linked insurance policies, mutual funds, UITFs and stocks.

5. Falling for investment scams. Scammers take advantage of the OFWs' burning desire to return home to their loved ones and not having to work away from them ever again. They make absurd promises of enormous earnings in a short period with minimal effort and position their investment as the best way towards getting rich. Sadly, many fall for these false promises. Do not allow criminals to steal your hard-earned money through dubious investment schemes. Before you put money in any investment, study it thoroughly and ask questions. Do not say yes to an investment immediately. Scammers usually persuade would-be victims to decide quickly so you won't have time to uncover their deception and lies. Think long and hard before deciding. Consult others who are knowledgeable about investing and familiar with what's being offered to you. If you have doubts about an investment then don't put your money in it. It's better for you to miss out on a legitimate investment with great returns because you had doubts than to lose your life's savings on a scam because you disregarded your doubts and instead believed their lies. Always keep in mind that if an investment is too good to be true, it's probably a scam!

6. Being overly generous with money. People who are

earning well tend to be more generous. Ever heard of the returning OFW who throws a feast not just for the family but for the whole neighborhood? Or the one who lavishes his family, relatives and friends with gifts in kind or in cash? There's nothing wrong with sharing your money as long as you do not over do it. Remember that there are more important uses for your money than making other people happy with cash. Be sensible when giving money. If you know that it's just going to be spent on non-essential items then don't give too much. Better yet give only when it is really needed. Also, be cautious in lending large amounts of money to people who intend to use it as capital for a business. Some relatives and friends of OFWs who do not have the knowledge, skills and right attitude to run a business suddenly feel like they are capable entrepreneurs knowing they can get money from the OFW. Do not lend money for capital unless you have the skill and competence to evaluate the would-be borrower's business plan and agree that it is feasible and profitable. The more money you have, the more relatives and friends will come to you asking for money. Learn to say "no!"

11

Don't Just Save, Invest!

Alvin T. Tabañag. RFP

www.pinoysmartsavers.com

The Fund Managers Association of the Philippines is celebrating its 14th founding anniversary this week, which is also being observed as "Investment Consciousness" week. This is a good time to remind everyone that saving is not enough – you have to learn to invest your money. Investing will help you "truly grow" your money and allow you to reach your financial goals faster.

What exactly do I mean by "truly grow?" It means that when you invest your money increases its real value. Compare this to putting, say P10,000, in a regular savings account that earns 1% per annum. At the end of one year your money may have grown to P10,100 (disregarding taxes) but it will actually buy less because prices of goods and services have increased more than 1%. In effect the real value of your money has decreased due to inflation. As a rule of thumb your money should be growing at least at the same rate as inflation so that it will not lose any purchasing value.

Investing not only helps you beat inflation but it will also help you grow your funds bigger and faster. By investing your funds you can meet your financial targets in half the time or even earlier. See below the increase in value of

P2,000 set aside monthly growing at different annual rates of return and the time it takes to reach P1M.

Period =   1% +   3% +   6% +   10% + 15%

5   years = 122T + 127T + 135T + 146T + 162T
10 years = 251T + 275T + 316T + 382T + 487T
15 years = 386T + 446T + 559T + 763T + 1.1M
20 years = 528T + 645T + 882T + 1.4M + 2.5M
25 years = 678T + 875T + 1.3M + 2.4M + 5.1M
30 years = 835T + 1.1M + 1.9M + 3.9M +10.4M

To P1M = 35yrs + 28yrs + 22yrs + 17yrs + 14yrs

If you put P2,000 monthly in a regular savings account that earns 1% per year, in 30 years you will only have P835T. But if you put the same amount in an investment that earns 6%, you will have P1.9M at the end of 30 years or P3.9M if it grows 10% yearly. That's a huge difference of P1.1M to P3.1M. Clearly, you will be losing out on a lot of money if you do not invest. Can you really afford to miss out on such a large sum of money?

I bet that the next question in your mind is "where the heck can my money earn 6% to 15% yearly?" Well, in more places than one. There are a number of investment products which can give you this much return (or even more) that have been around for quite some time. Consider investing in the following:

Long-term Time Deposit (TD) Accounts. Technically, it's not an investment vehicle but a savings product. However, it's still a good, effective and safe way for growing your money, especially if you are just starting out with investing. "Long-term" means TD accounts that mature in more than 5 years. Long-term TDs give the highest interest rates and interest earnings are exempt from the 20% withholding tax. If you look around you should be able to find banks that offer interest rates between 5 to 7% per annum.

Treasury Bills and Bonds. These are government-issued securities (GS) and can be acquired through banks and other non-bank entities. GS are virtually risk-free and earnings are guaranteed just like TDs. The minimum amount can be as low as P5,000 as in the case of retail treasury bonds (RTBs). To see the list of government securities eligible dealers go to

http://www.treasury.gov.ph/govsec/gsedlist.html.

Stocks. Investing directly in stocks is not for the faint-hearted because stock values can swing wildly within a matter of days or weeks. (If you can still take it easy when the value of your stocks drops 5 to 10% in one day, then stock investing can be for you.) Although stock growth is not guaranteed, good stocks have been known to perform very well over the long term. To learn more about investing in stocks go to

http://www.pse.com.ph/html/InvestingInPSE/investing_pse.html.

You can also try the Philippine Stocks Exchange online stock trading simulation game (http://www.pse.ph/html/STG/index.html) for a safe and fun way to **get you going with investing in the stock market.**

Mutual Funds and Unit Investment Trust Funds (UITFs). If you have limited funds but want to have access to the growth potential of a greater number of different stocks and investments products, try investing in mutual funds and UITFs. These are pooled funds invested in a mix of government securities & other fixed-income instruments, stocks and/or the money market. These are popular among more knowledgeable savers due to their potential for higher returns. Mutual funds and UITFs come in different varieties (equity, bond, balanced and money-market) with different levels of risk and growth potential. A fund's value is constantly changing and may go up or down. Thus, growth is not guaranteed and you may lose some of your capital. Historically though, most funds have clearly outpaced inflation over the long term. The average 5-year return of all equity mutual funds in the Philippines is 16%.

View the historical performance of all mutual funds at http://www.icap.com.ph/factsfignavps.asp.
To learn more about mutual funds visit
http://www.icap.com.ph/mf_101.html.
For more information about UITFs and the banks offering them go to http://www.uitf.com.ph/.

Other investment vehicles. Of course there are other ways to grow your money like real estate, life insurance products, pre-need plans, forex trading and running your own business. We'll cover that in other article.

The best time to start investing is today. Each day of delay will cost you in potential earnings. You might think that you will need a large amount of money before you can invest. Wrong! You can start investing with P10,000 or even less. Visit a bank, mutual fund company or stock broker today and ask about their investment options. You'll be surprised at how little it takes to get started and launch your journey towards financial success.

12

MRT-3: The Daily Commute Is The Destination

Resty Odon

(I am a long-time freelance magazine contributor and blogger writing on various topics, from travel to birdwatching to psychospirituality toFilipino life to anything I consider quirky enough to merit my attention. I blog at http://restyo.blogspot.com)

Dateline, Feb 22, 2007

The first time I took the MRT, I had this feeling I wasn't in the danged P.I. All that gleaming metal, newly manufactured rubber, squeaky escalators... It was like putting a new car to a test drive - it's a novelty that would stay with me for a very long time. I felt like the robot character in the movie Short Circuit where, the moment he's trundled out of the lab and into the great wide open, he is overwhelmed by what he sees that all he could say is an ecstatic, "Input!," "Input!," as his digital eyes record everything in sight.

I would seldom take the MRT after that. There was no need to, except when I had to be in Cubao from Ayala in split seconds. It was years later, when I would leave my job in the comfort zone of Makati and find a new one in faraway Q.C. that I became an MRT regular. Becoming a regular would eventually mean becoming what you might call an MRT addict. That meant taking the train twice a day. That meant regarding the MRT experience in a whole new way.

The two-way ride, needless to say, soon ceased to be a novelty. It turned into something familiar which, as familiarity goes, I anticipated to view with contempt. Yet, strangely, so far, after about two months' commute, I couldn't bring myself to being my old contemptuous self. For a born pessimist, that's a lot. My five-day-a-week MRT commute would prove to be something I am grateful of as a much-needed improvement, a breath of fresh air, in my Third World existence as a commuter.

Day to day, I step into coach after coach with this cocktail of oft-clashing, sometimes-cryptic feelings. But whichever the case, the result is always something delicate. First, there's the nostalgia I associate with the whole thing. I happen to have personally known this PR guy assigned to handle the public affairs side of this monstrous to-do that was this behemoth's construction at the time. I remember how all of us who used EDSA went through months, even years, of hell for it that, we thought, "It better be damn serviceable, or else, there'd be hell to pay…"

Thank goodness there soon arose in this corner of EDSA (Pasay Rd./Aranaiz Ave.) this giant billboard to allay our inner suicide bomber. "Cubao to Makati in 15 minutes!" said the poster, my friend the PR guy's brainchild, no doubt. It employed a generic-looking, street-smart construction guy as an MRT poster boy. This, in between the neon lights at night blinking, "Safety First!," if not "Please bear with us" or "Your taxes are working for you." I'm not sure which part worked, but the PR gimmick would in no time receive recognition in an international PR awards ceremony in Finland a year or so after.

Far from inspiring contempt, this giant caterpillar ride

soon made me regard it with fondness, the way I would have for an extended ride in the roller caosters at Enchanted Kingdom (our local version of Disneyland, in Sta. Rosa, Laguna). I thought they might as well install a 360-degree loop in the middle of Magallanes, overlooking the Skyway on the SLEX or in Cubao where the MRT intersects LRT2. To complete the circus feel, they could add a series of horror trains perhaps at the Buendia and Ayala stations, which are actually tunnels or practically the closest we could ever get to a subway. For someone given to thinking exquisitely pompous thoughts and spectacularly implausible scenarios at lucid intervals, the MRT ride is such a welcome opportunity.

It's also something that offers a little complexity to my embarrassingly simple, regular life, even as I am transported with ease from point A to point B. I could be catching myself between paraphrasing Pico Iyer thoughts ("To travel is to taste hardship.") and faintly anticipating someone in the crowd yelling "Emergency!" Or I could be testing the effect of viewing the entire length of EDSA with this and that techno or punk rock accompaniment, as played in my brother's iPod. As I meditate deep stuff, I am forced to multi-task: Often, it's all about getting myself stuck between not just two interesting people but also equally exquisite dilemmas. For example: (a) getting irked by a seatmate who coughs nonstop and smells of freshly pounded garlic and (b) repositioning my eye sockets to avoid staring directly at the vicinity of people's knees. The thing is, there is great unpredictability amid all that regularity, and this is what probably keeps the MRT ride from ever becoming boring, at least for me.

Soon enough, as the train moves you along its track with First-World regularity, you will be forced to notice a lot of other things outside the window, too, that you had taken for granted before. Oftentimes you find yourself both being literally and figuratively taken for an MRT ride. You notice that those hotels painted in Day-Glo colors are the gaudiest buildings in the Metro, and also its ugliest. You also notice those chintzy, glinting tiled roofs of Corinthian Garden and Blue Ridge mansions, and wonder whether everybody, each and every Filipino, would ever afford to have one such in their lifetime. You notice how, with Imee Marcos' smirk (or is that a pout? or is that a British stiff upper lip?), Borgy Manotoc's giant mug in a Swatch billboard on the Robinson's Galleria mall's façade is staring down at the brass statue of Our Lady of EDSA with impunity.

If weirder thoughts assault you without any warning, it's because you can afford all that luxury. One time, from out of the blue, it occurs to me that the solution to the constant traffic in EDSA is a very simple one: Let those who go to Makati and Pasay for their jobs swap houses and apartments with those coming from Quezon City and its environs. Makes a lot of sense to me.

An MRT ride also means disorientation in minutes, which closely resembles the effect one feels traveling by plane. Working in Quezon City these days is a culture shock for someone who has worked in Makati all his life. Q.C., though home of the biggest TV media players ABS-CBN and GMA7, seems to be more of an NGO and bureaucrat haven to me, so far removed from the glass-tower realities I've known and gotten used to. Now, I'm no longer certain which of the two nerve centers of the metro has more...er, character.

It's a difference in the look-and-feel that I didn't notice much before, which I notice now because I perceive what's supposed to be a subtle change in just a matter of minutes instead of the usual time gap you get (hours and hours!) by traveling by car or bus. That familiar time gap is suddenly bridged by the efficacious speed of the trains. You discern something that's indefinably lost behind all that efficiency.

Before the MRT, it took an entire desert caravan-paced expedition for one to reach Novaliches from Taft Ave., Pasay City. The hours-long time lag that mentally and physically prepares the traveler that he/she is going to another, different place is lost, together with the psychological presumption that one is traveling from one place that's very familiar and contemptible to another that's far and a bit strange and perhaps much more inviting.

An MRT ride engenders that unique vision of this slice of city life, something which cannot be replicated by any other experience, I'm afraid, unless perhaps they build new lines like this. (Phase 2 will reportedly extend this line to Monumento, in Caloocan.) I wonder what happens if everything moved this fast; will all the necessary changes soon follow and make the whole megalopolis melt in a bland uniformity?

As a lot of people know, the Metro Rail Transit was built by a consortium under a build-operate-transfer scheme during President Fidel V. Ramos's administration to the tune of $655-million. MRTC is led by Fil-Estate and composed of Ayala Land Inc., Anglo-Philippine Holdings, Ramcar Greenfield Development, Allante Realty and DBH Inc. The MRT-3 Blue Line, also known as Metrostar Express, spans 6.4 km. of EDSA, punctuated at irregular intervals by 13 stations that offer vantage points that vary, not the least in height and the views available.

There's the treetop-level (Annapolis-Santolan), the street level (Pasay-Taft), the subterranean (Ayala Ave.), the mangy and grungy (Cubao), the billboard-choked (Guadalupe). It was reported that the roughly 30-minute ride has a present "ridership" of about 400,000 per day. At this point, it might be interesting to compare and contrast the MRT with the LRT if only to further point out something I missed so far: While LRT1 cuts right through the middle of all that Old World civilization, with its horrors of postcolonial decay and patches of hopeful rebirth and awful remodeling, MRT gives a more comprehensive picture of, say, the New World, albeit in a little more distant, a little less in-your-face manner. Cruising the city on the more intimate level of the LRT ride, you get to meet the earthiest urban characters at odd hours, intimate enough for you to exchange your face with somebody else, like this ambulant vendor I had met who had this intrusive prerecorded sales pitch that played, "Mura lang, mura lang, piso isa, piso isa...," the tape being in an unending repeat mode. That sort of visceral thing. I once gave a man-on-the-street LRT tour guide to a visitor from California a cousin asked me to show around, and his reaction was all of a nervous, wide-eyed, and diplomatic "It's pretty packed!"

You won't hear that kind of social commentary with MRT travel, even when the rush-hour traffic slams you with a tsunami of warm bodies getting ready for coffee and perhaps a nasty inter-office memo. At the maximum cost of P14 (one-way), you get an entire panorama of a grimy, topsy-turvy, unplaceable, fairly cosmopolitan metropolis, one that's strangely capable of summoning the entire gamut of emotions from you.

This relatively new slithering landmark of the city does all these things I just told you about -- and perhaps more.

Well, for instance, it also makes you assess -- from some sort of a rarefied vantage point -- how life in the P.I. is, after those four fateful days of February 1986 that stunned the whole world, the longest days this country ever had.

***

Some tips to maximize the benefits of your MRT trip:

1. Don't wear a miniskirt. If you're a guy, always be sure you didn't leave your fly open.
2. For the best deal, buy the P100 'stored-value' card. It saves time, and you get to avail of bonus rides.
3. Bring no bags or anything that could invite suspicion.
4. Never take a seat if you are given to being attacked by pangs of guilt.
5. Avoid the rush hours: 8-9AM and 6-7 PM and these chokepoints as point of entry: Guadalupe, Cubao, Pasay Rotunda and North Ave. stations.
6. Avoid the doors at all costs to avoid the onrush and in case of stampede.
7. But if you 'travel' for the pain and inconvenience, go park yourself right at the door.

13

Manila: A Glorious Mismatch - A Happy Confusion

Resty Odon

From his blog:
Dateline, Sept 30, 2010

(This is Side B, in answer to that other offending article by someone, "Disorientation in Manila.")

Where can you find a place where Chinese gargoyles pose together with aquiline-nosed saints in white stone? Where American World War II cars are pimped up pre-MTV, choking the sidestreets cheek by jowl with rickety horse drawn carriages from a bygone era? Where Korean bubblegum pop competes with Justin Bieber or a spoofed version of any of the latest from American Top 40? Where basketball, boxing, beauty contests, pork stew, grilled chicken, and tear-jerking television soaps reign as cultural icons? Where else but in Manila, where the weird genetic makeup results in a lot of mismatches that both confound and delight?

Whenever I am asked about my favorite place in the Philippines, I always have one answer ready. My inquisitors are, of course, distraught, demanding to know why I didn't answer Boracay, Bohol, Baguio, Tagaytay, Cebu, Banawe or or Sagada. Why indeed choose such a sprawl of poured concrete on which live and breathe its pullulating inhabitants? I am nonetheless unnerved by such quizzical reactions because I am ever-ready to support my claim – it's just that I can't explain in neat sentences, for I am swamped with concrete evidence.

The real Manila is not the Manila people read in the news. My Manila is a place of hidden excitement waiting to fascinate those whose interest lies beyond beachbumming.
It may look drab and square on the surface, it's true, but the wise would do well not to be fooled by what's apparent. As omnipresent Manila-phile Carlos Celdran puts it, "We don't put on a show here." Yeah -- not our style.

My own private experience of my favorite spot on the planet has consistently pointed to one fact: Manila is simply the most cosmopolitan place I've ever known, and I don't even have to exert an effort. There is always a strong element of the unexpected, and in endless variety too. I was born in Manila, but spent most of my growing up years in the country from age 6 onwards, but being a Manila boy never left me. I constantly longed for the lure of the place. I knew I'd be back someday. True enough, when I returned to be a resident once again, I hungrily made up for lost time by taking in its soul – its sights, sounds, smells – digging every corner for finds. Manila never changed, I found. When I got past its being maximally designed to offend, annoy, or harass both inhabitant and visitor, past the seeming earnestness to become a showcase of social injustice in the Philippines, it has proven to be the same inebriating cocktail of cultures that I expected it to have, only this time even better.

Note that I am not talking about forced cosmopolitanism. I am talking about an authenticity anyone can observe in a typical Manila folk on the street patronizing everything even without the benefit of advertising. What the ignorant is quick to label as an unpretty outpost in the 'Far East,' those in the know will only laugh off dismissively, for they know that Manila has always been like this throughout its colorful history.

Admittedly, writers don't exactly wax poetic and novelists seldom choose it for their setting, but those in the know won't balk at the idea. Pierre Cardin, no less than the famous French figure of haute couture, was certainly in the know when, in his visit, he immediately pronounced the city to be "an old civilization" and lauded its residents for being "cosmopolitan." Now there's an unbiased cue for everybody.

The uninitiated will be surprised to know that, behind the Philippine capital's bloody history, is a glorious story of global exposure, albeit at certain times bloody. Native son Nick Joaquin has duly noted this in his book *Manila My Manila*, i.e., how Manila Bay with its famed sunset turned this city into an economic crossroads, a cradle of global trade long before globalization became a buzzword. Its history of conquest by three imperial powers (four if we include the two-year British invasion) certainly enriched the city's cultural life with layers of influences.

To think that Manila was almost expunged out of existence in WWII. Old Manila almost never recovered its original racial mix and the exchange of goods, glances, and who knew what else that ensued. (War records would routinely turn up with unlikely foreign nationalities such Germans, Portuguese, and French among the casualties; there was even a report of a Jewish synagogue somewhere along Taft.) But the city eventually expanded into a Greater Manila that continues to gobble up everything that it touches up to this day, continuously adding regional influences on top of an already thick palimpsest.

Here's my very own view of the city, in segments, as a place where unexpected juxtapositions not just catch me by surprise but actually cause what they call "unintended beauty."

Architecture

Despite the prewar damage, a few defining structures remain, resulting in visual diversity, albeit constantly endangered by the wrecker's ball. (But thanks to the effort of intrepid groups like Ivan Henares' Heritage Conservation Society, Manila's heritage hemorrhage may be stanched yet.) Name an era in Philippine history and you'll find a few standing markers, architecturally speaking. With Josefina P. Manahan's *Streetbound: Manila on Foot* (2001) as guide, I've seen first-hand the beauty of the Spanish-Mexican colonial baroque (Quiapo Church), bahay na bato (the Hispanized version of nipa hut, in Intramuros), beaux arts (Luneta Hotel), art deco (Metropolitan Theater), art nouveau (ancestral houses in Quiapo), neoclassical (the wedding cake-like Post Office), palazzos, neogothic (San Beda), Streamline Moderne (Far Eastern University), Marcos-era/New Society commissioned 'building sculptures' (Cultural Center, an abstracted version of the nipa hut), the Bauhaus (Ayala Tower One, Philamlife Tower, Enterprise Center, all in Makati; the new highrises in Fort Bonifacio, Taguig).

These structures make Manila a giant time machine for me. That Rizal Ave. corner where gorgeous neoclassical, baroque, and art deco buildings from different periods in history desperately try to survive feels like looking at a patient in the ICU, a sad/beautiful moment. I never know what will happen next. The Post Office, on the other hand, sits on the Pasig River bank, Parthenon-like, with such permanence, but with the flair of an eye-catching drama queen. The once-defunct and now being restored Metropolitan Theater is absolutely whimsical, but with class/restraint, its unforgettable structure and exquisite details the kind your eyes won't ever tire of. The Luneta Hotel is equally interesting for its aura of French aristocracy. In stark contrast, Leandro Locsin's Cultural Center of the Philippines is perhaps the architectural equivalent of a Mondrian painting. Notably, too, the resultant patina of dignity, the verdigris of gracious ageing, can be easily mistaken for urban squalor, which admittedly comes aplenty side by side the spanking new.

I've gathered the above personal observations from the current architectural and history walk tours I've either seen in passing or actually tried and thus highly recommend: Carlos Celdran's tour of Intramuros, Quiapo, etc.; Ivan Man-Dy's tours of Binondo, Chinese Cemetery, FEU, and the neogothic area of San Miguel; and Lawrence Chan's postal history tour. Each of these tours is an enriching experience, especially for a history and culture trivia buff like me.

Churches

I am especially fond of ancient temples, and my favorites among the colonial churches in the country are all found here: the neogothic San Sebastian Church, a prefab all steel structure shipped from Belgium, and the bizarre San Agustin Church, which is painted inside in the elaborate Italian trompe l'oeil style, and the Paco Church and Cemetery, which totally weirds me out.

The San Sebastian church is a marriage of steel with the gothic design idiom, a structure arising from Old Manila's decaying streetscape like a pleasant surprise.

The San Agustin church, the country's oldest stone church (completed in 1607), and its adjoining museum has a misleadingly simple exterior hiding an intricately breathtaking interior. Here, I get to stand on the lapidas of Manila's founder Miguel Lopez de Legaspi et al, literally. The only survivor of that tragic WWII American-Japanese bombardment of Intramuros, this place has been a repository of an unbelievable collection of disembodied ivory heads of saints that look Chinese but are dressed as Spanish.

This strange combo meal is repeated in front and elsewhere: blackened Chinese gargoyles (called fu or guard 'dogs' (lions?) in granite) in front of blinding-white, aquiline-nosed saints from Europe, etc. Among the most precious artifacts are the frames of pressed plant leaves originally belonging to the country's first botanist, Fray Manuel Blanco, an Augustinian. The dark choir loft stuns in the dark, with its ornately hand-carved chairs made of molave, echoing the elegant main door, and a humongous cantoral (music guidebook) with Gregorian chant notes.

The Paco Church and Cemetery, with its unique circular structure and such a dark history of massive death and destruction, is now a place of concerts and beautiful weddings/receptions -- a happy irony!

In Quiapo, there is a Muslim mosque with a golden sheen and an old and really quirky Japanese pagoda featuring add-on details best suited to a medieval European castle. Add one gigantic Virgin Mary santo inside and that amusing halo-halo feeling is complete.

I especially love Binondo, Manila's Chinatown, for its unbelievable melding of three (or more) ancient cultural influences, as condensed, for example, in the little worship corner called Cristo de Longos along Tomas Pinpin cor. Ongpin, where devotees burn joss sticks and whisper petitions to a wooden cross reportedly sourced from Mexico.

Food

Manila's appetite is not widely known, but it should be. Manila's culinary attractions cater to any budget, from shoestring/backpacker to high-end. A cursory trip to Manila's streets, malls, and resto strips will reveal diverse cuisines, both regional and international, all striving to be authentic. The variety improves year by year that, today, one can run to specialty houses for Ilocano, Ilonggo, Pampango, or Quezon comfort foods as well as Chinese, Japanese, Vietnamese, Singaporean, Malaysian, Thai, Indian, American, Australian, Mexican, Spanish, French, Italian, Korean, and Middle Eastern cuisines. For an otherwise humid and grungy-looking metropolis that's classified as "Third World," that's far too remarkable.

Imagine my delight, for instance, when I randomly bumped into one Mexican restaurant (Cantina) that offered a "Mexican inasal." I couldn't decide whether I wanted to be in Guadalajara or Mexico. The latest food fad to hit the city is 'froyo' fever (frozen yoghurt), and I am gladly 'infected.' I frequent the Dad's-Kamayan-Saisaki buffet, but my enduring favorites are the little cafeteria style

Chinese eateries in Binondo (Tasty Dumpling for its fried porkchop and steamed vegetable dumplings and winter melon juice, Wai-Ying for its braised duck and radishcake, etc.) and authentic Greek food at Cyma, where they serve saganaki and other delicious flambéed numbers with a loud cry of "Opa!" For this issue, we held a random toss-up of the excellent fine-dining places (apart from the LJC chain of names, that is, which are consistently of top quality), and we had Zuni (Continental-Mediterranean) and Chateau 1771 ("borderless cuisine") at Greenbelt 5.

Museums

Another of Manila's best-kept secrets is its world-class museums. Stunning is the only apt word I could think of to describe their acquisitions. My favorite showcases include the National Museum and the Museum of the Filipino People across the street, where all the rarest and most valuable cultural and natural treasures of the archipelago are housed under one roof: Juan Luna's "Spoliarium," the Manunggul burial jar, Calatagan clay pot, Laguna copper plate, Jose Rizal's boyhood sculptures, and other attractions that help define the hazy Filipino identity. One Sunday, I ran into tour guide Rommel Garcia giving a lecture on the famed paintings to visiting students from Poveda. I listened in and absorbed certain art and history tidbits I'd never learn anywhere.

If I want to further feel good about being Filipino, I go to the Metropolitan Museum for their vast collection of precolonial gold jewelry and other unique finds. I get astounded by ancient glitters and surprisingly advanced level of craftsmanship (circa 9th century). I am especially enamored of the "Niño Dormido," a depiction of the sleeping Child Jesus in ivory encased in glass with fine gold lace embellishments of Chinese influence.

This is part of the Draper Loot, according to the Met Museum's May Cruz, recovered by Jaime Laya of the Central Bank from a Sotheby's auction. Cruz echoes my thoughts as she wonders aloud how much else of that loot from the two-year British invasion (1760-1762), which brought us the British Indian Sepoys now dwelling in Cainta, Rizal, is still out there waiting to be reclaimed. This museum piece is singularly striking for its supreme irony: a supposedly poor God-child as helpless human royalty.

The Ayala Museum's own precolonial gold collection looks like an extension of the Central Bank's, and it is even more spectacular! I had to breathlessly note down these items to be among its highly unusual acquisitions: a pair of garuda (Hindu-Buddhist mythical bird) earrings, a kinnari goddess (outsize-breasted half-woman, half-swan vessel), a simple pure-gold offertory bowl, a highly original outlandishly designed death mask, exquisitely carved hilts, elaborate woven wear for the wrist and hips, and a baldric (shoulder belt used for carrying weapon), among other arresting finds. Together with the history dioramas, loaned costumes from the Netherlands, and boat replicas, these items make the Ayala Museum a must-see, with each exihibition deserving a separate feature.

Casa Manila is yet another stunner among Manila's underpublicized museums. Upon entry to the museum, one sees a rather nonpicturesque to drab patio, in marked contrast to the marvels that await the visitor inside. This stark lack of dramatics creates the same effect when you enter the San Agustin Church across the road: the intentional lack of cues or clues (clue-lessness?) outside only heightens the breathtaking surprise of the interior. Designed to be a replica of the typical home of the hacendero-ilustrado, the casa's Spanish baroque is combined with the two-story bahay kubo (nipa hut) design, but with two additional distinctions often left out in the usual description: the furniture pieces are mostly American (not Spanish), mostly in the art nouveau style, with the pervading darkness of ebony (molave wood) lending an unintentionally gothic look. Some Chinese chests and ceramics punctuate the darkness with some color. This little-known trade we had with Boston, Massachusetts, and Salem, Pennsylvania, at the time is identified to be responsible for the American influence long before the actual American occupation. The foreigner, the Filipino elite, and the *indio hampaslupa* (e.g., me) will surely have widely divergent views of the casa spectacle. A carpeted and heavily guarded (by guardia civils, who else) walk-through is a veritable parade review of homestyling terms we have largely discarded: from the *zaguan* (corridor) to the *entresuelo* (tenant waiting room), to the *despacho* (landlord's office), *caida* (antesala), *cuartos* (bedrooms), *sala* (living room), *oratorio* (prayer room), *comedor* (dining room), *cocina* (kitchen), *letrina* (latrine), *baño* (bathroom), and *azotea* (second-story porch). We have here either a source of pride in our cultural legacy or heritage and a cause of possible distress for those who happen to see only the impossibility of living up to such a benchmark, if we may call the highest standards we have achieved ages ago a benchmark.

Music

Manila sound is hard to peg down, "but it's there," as prodigious composer Ryan Cayabyab once put it. It's there in multiple genres, with a band playing in some lounge or dive their chosen specialty, be it jazz, metal, ska, RnB, punk, rap/hip-hop, or reggae. There was a time when my favorite radio station was LA 104.9, which gave me a glimpse of the world's music, from Afropop to zydeco. It's now gone, but the restless enthusiast in me remains sated. The fads of late have been bossa nova and Korean bubblegum pop plus J-pop and Taiwanese acts. I am lucky to be a spectator, having been a part-time music reviewer, struggling to be detached and objective, as I saw most acts live, such as Apo Hiking Society, Martin Nievera, Bamboo, Itchyworms, Hale, Up Dharma Down, Pedicab, Gloc9, MYMP, Cookie Chua, Drip, Sarah Geronimo, Christian Bautista, and Freestyle. With the advent of iPod and illegal downloads, it's anybody's guess what Manilans like me are up to.

Film

Manileños' film appreciation has likewise evolved through the years. I've been a long-time fan of foreign filmfests, with Manila's resident embassies giving us an opportunity to view films from places as disparate as Finland, Brazil, Indonesia, Poland, etc. This adds an exciting novelty to what's been dubbed as third golden age (i.e., these days) in Philippine filmmaking, spurred on by rising indie artists, a lot of them based in Manila.

Plays

Manila is also a place to go for world-class plays staged by heroic (because underfunded) theater groups that have produced the likes of Lea Salonga and others.

Showbiz

The Philippine capital also happens to be where the major TV and film studios are, so a trip to, say, ABS-CBN and GMA7 to witness popular shows like "Wowowee" and its variants and see gorgeous stars in the flesh is, without a question, included in my to-do list. Manila's beautiful people can be its most compelling attraction, and can be the world's most gorgeous and charming, too, what with the variously mixed-race beauty increasing in diversity with each passing year (as only befits an embracing society as the Filipinos'). It's always unforgettable encountering export-quality pulchritude in the flesh everywhere in the metropolis. Yes, they all live and breathe here like we all do. As John Mayer drawled, "[They] look so good it hurts sometimes."

Shopping

From tiangges in Greenhils, Divisoria, and Baclaran, to the Weekend Markets in Salcedo, Legaspi, and Magallanes (Makati), Ortigas, and QC, to the giant malls (SM North, Megamall, Mall of Asia), Manila has also been a shopping paradise even to this hesitant shopper who hates shopping and weekend crowds. My favorite malls are the elegantly designed malls of the Ayalas: Greenbelt, Glorietta, and Serendra, especially that strip called Bonifacio High Street. I also frequent the back of the Mall of Asia, a splendid location to watch the changing moods of the sea and the constant shifting of the clouds (those "ice-cream castles in the sky"!).

Parks

If not pockmarked with hellholes and choked by giant billboards, pedicaps and tricycles, Manila is essentially Skimpyton. Huge parks are few and far between, so each one is precious to me, from Luneta (Rizal Park) to Ninoy Aquino Parks and Wildlife to La Mesa Ecopark to the University of the Philippines' greenery, including the Sunken Garden, in Diliman. In the Ninoy Aquino Parks and Wildlife lagoon, groups of artists park their easels in the area and will sketch your likeness in charcoal for free if you're lucky. Because I am also a bird watching hobbyist, another haunt is the American Cemetery at Fort Bonifacio, which exudes an almost soundless, otherworldly air amidst the manicured greens. Binoculars in hand, I once joined Michael Lu and the Wild Bird Club of the Philippines in spotting endemic birds, such as the *kilyawan* (an oriole) and *kulasisi* (a parrot), whose calls pierced the tranquility in staccatos. Though not exactly a park, the Manila Ocean Park is likewise highly recommended, being a world-class oceanarium befitting an anchipelago of dwarfism and gigantism: the world's longest coastline harboring both the smallest and largest marine species.

Sports

When it comes to sports, Manila is also synonymous to the Araneta Coliseum where epic matches between university rivals, the Ateneo Blue Eagles and De La Salle Green Archers, are much-anticipated, not to mention the equally popular professional team matches often held at the Cuneta Astrodome. There is always an infectious spirit that goes with these matches, even if I only find myself being trapped in the MRT together with all the hard-core Atenean and La Sallite fans. This infection was recently caught overseas by American author Bartholomew who came to town and wrote an entire book on it.

Meanwhile, Manny Pacquiao sightings here and there, becoming increasingly rare, are also routine headline news among Manilans.

There are many other things I love about Manila. There used to be a time when a jeepney ride inside the Nayong Pilipino park meant a microcosmic tour of the Philippine Islands. That's sadly gone, but I refuse to "speak of Manila in past tense," to steal somebody's quote, for there are simply so many other things to like. Catching a glimpse of the giant orange ball descending on the horizon while I'm inside the LRT always reduces me into a pair of two big orbs. In La Salle Taft, University Belt, UP, University of

Santo Tomas, and the Ateneo, shamelessly ogling at the country's future best and brightest, at their most beautiful stage in life, is always an infectious joy. (Manila should have a walk tour of all these school campuses.) Lunchbreak at the Enterprise Center, LKG Tower, or PBCom Bldg's Patio along Ayala Ave. gives me a good feel of the office and BPO crowd in Makati, the country's new financial district (the old being Binondo). A limited glimpse of Malacañang Palace inside an air-con catamaran down the Pasig feels like an exercise in voyeurism against a Php20 bill. The beautiful modern structures arising like mushrooms in The Fort in Taguig smell of the future of Manila, which is to say, bright, prosperous, and clean. A glimpse of the life of the rich and famous inside the most exclusive gated villages. The lights and lanterns along Ayala Ave. on Christmas never fail to enchant me back into a devoted believer in visual magic. The other peculiar spots I am especially fond of because I bonded with them the most as a toddler, kid, and preteen include Manila Zoo, Luneta, Fort Santiago, Harrison Plaza, Paco public market, Pandacan, and Araneta Center in Cubao (Araneta Coliseum, Ali Mall, Rustans, COD), all reminding me of personal moments with my mother, aunts, and cousins, all containing untold personal stories. The list goes on and on and on, but surprise... I never get to repeat myself or tire myself off it. In cosmopolitan Manila, I am instead deliriously disorientated.

(A shorter version of this article was published in Asian Traveler magazine in October 2010. Acknowledgement: Nash Vendeville, Rommel Cruz (National Museum), Intramuros Administration, Rinnah Sevilla (Ayala Museum), May Cruz (Metropolitan Museum), Cyrus Cruz and Lucille Robinson (Chateau 1771), Andy Atienza (Zuni).

14

Triptych

Resty Odon

1. Weirdoes in a Weird Land

Who are we? Good question, because there are no straight answers. But if we believe that a clinical examination of ourselves is necessary to get the best answer, then we need a SWOT analysis of the Filipino. This self-accounting is expected to lead us to the truth, not self-congratulatory self-delusions. Let's get started.

What are Filipinos? Well, we're a weird people living in a weird land. That's pretty much apparent from the get-go. Geographically and biologically, we are a land of giants and dwarves: smallest volcano, smallest primate, biggest fish, etc. We're also a major diversity hotspot. Culturally, the contrasts and diversity are equally bizarre: We're a Babel of tongues, a confusion of genes.

Here's some more: We're the only predominantly Christian nation in Asia. Its most democratic nation. Its freest press. An "anomaly" even in the literary scene.

This question then begs to be asked: How could a speck of Asian dust hold not just miniature life but also immensities and diversities? Weird, right? But we never intended to come up with such incredible coincidences. No, we don't put up a good show here. The Engineer of the universe must have bestowed it upon us:

"Thou art meant to be weird." The irony is, we aren't as aware, as concerned, or as proud as we should be for the distinction. In fact, we're too embarrassed for being "differently interesting."

2. People of Paradox

We Flips are people of "seeming contradictions." Note how our cuisine is not as particular with the presentation, but more about the taste. We're after what's essential, not superficial. When it comes to personal physical appearances, however, it's amazing how we're totally vain. We are an image-driven, status-conscious society. We are supposed to be open-minded to a fault. This makes us such notorious copycats. But that also means we have a predilection for eclectic designs, cosmopolitan choices. We don't frown upon inter-racial marriages. We even readily embraced the religion of our conquerors – but that's by choice.

Puzzlingly, this openness would give us a ferocious hatred of empty spaces (horror vacui). We couldn't possibly suffer from claustrophobia, ever. We're in love with borloloy. Yet beneath the sheen of Pacific Islander gaudiness and ostentation, don't we betray something dark? What's the point of our love affair with plural word forms, raucous fiestas, and baroque extraneousness? Is it because we've always been lustful for life, or is it because we've always felt deprived?

Whatever it is, everything has to be crammed inside our soul, including whatever Zen minimalism we may have absorbed through Japanese osmosis. This has prompted Conrado de Quiros to pronounce, "We are nothing and everything," in answer to the question, "What is a Filipino?" Krip Yuson is less sure, though: "Are we a palimpsest or a tabula rasa?," he wonders.

Thanks to our colonial history, perhaps, we seem to be at home with tight situations and dire straits. In the middle of coups and economic collapses, we choose to kibitz and grin before the camera. This fatalism may indicate not just a strong faith, but also a certain level of humility and honesty. We don't have a traditional fixation for being the 'mostest' or the 'winningest,' unless we're being selfdeprecating.

What we have, according to Nick Joaquin, is an appalling "heritage of smallness." But aren't we fond of playing pretend just the same? Aren't we masters not merely of pretentiousness, but of pretensions? Aren't we widely known for being onionskinned and non-confrontational hile we are brutishly frank behind others' back just the same?

We haven't contributed a single invention that's probably more earth-shaking than the yo-yo. But we have supplied the world with a prodigious number of maids, whose services, if terminated simultaneously would, as humorist Jessica Zafra theorizes, trigger a global crisis. Someone less jocose and more positive-thinking has countered, "It's because we are busy with revolutions, writing Asia's first constitution, building Asia's first republic, allowing women's suffrage for the first time in Asia, etc., etc., that's why."

What can we possibly say at this point, but that we're truly a paradox? The litany can go on and on, a list that can only drive us into the conceit that someone somewhere has written us down as being chosen. "Lo, we are the chosen people of Asia," some would say now and then. When you think about it, didn't we indeed entitle our national anthem "Lupang Hinirang"? Isn't Juan dela Cruz, our national nickname, the John of the Cross of Carmelite mysticism?

Indeed, in keeping with that theme, we currently have our own version of the Exodus and the Diaspora. Like the Jews say, being a 'chosen people' comes with a high price. It makes perfect sense then that we are tagged as the Asian Jews.

But if we have been chosen, it mustn't be because we're special, but because we're a deeply flawed, inconsistent people. At worst, we're simply illogical, but, at best, we might well be - you guessed it - paradoxical.

3. What We Are Not

It's kind of perverse to seek validation from other people's failures, but truth can come out from most unlikely places. Consider the following:

We don't have a legacy of war atrocities that we deny to our last dying breath, promising to forever embarrass our kinds. We don't gang-rape prepubescent girls and call them comfort food. We don't have imperialist dreams hanging over the whole of Asia.

Our nation hasn't been divided by any arbitrary parallel line, wall, iron curtain, or sea of conflicting ideologies – and we're not endlessly arguing over whose side is legitimate.

We didn't invent such buzzwords as concentration camp, gulag, gas chamber, genocide. Instead of turning each other into kebab, our ethnic groups tend to swap DNAs. We may be status-conscious, but we never devolved into a virulent caste system, the kind that condemns certain unfortunate folks as 'untouchable.' We didn't have to deal with the shame of apartheid.

We never institutionalized decapitation as punishment. Many of us want the death penalty abolished. We don't murder people just because they're Chinese or Buddhist or Muslim. Not a single would-be saint has been known to have been martyred here because it's just not our style. Our government does not sponsor terrorism. We don't have a state religion as official policy. We don't have a gene pool with the mind-boggling diversity of a cornfield. We have complemented our looks with lots of outside strains and we're not complaining about the improvement. We can chew bubble gum to our heart's content and not be jailed or rattan-caned for it. We can criticize our public officials and, normally, we don't get behind bars for it. Our diet is relatively healthy and not too spicy as to bring armpits to boiling point and test people's patience and endurance.

Normally, we do not separate the sexes in public spaces. Men and/or women can openly look at women and/or men in admiration. We don't subject our women to genital mutilation, force them into garbs that render them invisible, like Harry Potter's magic cloak, as though they're offensive as sin.

We may be materialistic, but our social network is not so heartless and dehumanizing as to drive our elderly to nursing homes. We may be fearful of authority and tend to avoid confrontation, but it also means we're respectful. We don't have to suffer snowstorms, twisters, sandstorms, and the freezing cold of winter, nor search for an oasis in the middle of the desert. We need not import water or desalinize the Pacific just to quench our thirst. Tropical weather makes us sweat a lot, too, so we bathe a lot and smell good even as we detoxify.

We are far less parochial. We're truly multicultural: there's a successful fusion of cultures in our way of life, and not merely a group of different cultures trying so hard to live in peaceful coexistence - or is it maximum tolerance. Our national identity may be sketchy at best or confused at worst, yet it remains uniquely, inimitably Filipino. Our colonial mentality is tempered by our penchant to 'Filipinize' the foreign, thus we end up conquering our own colonizers, preserving whatever is left of our flimsy indigenous side.

We can laugh at anything, especially at our own personal tragedies. Foreign surveys have repeatedly shown that we are happier than most people in Asia, though we're a lot poorer. We have a far lower suicide rate.

In 1986, we kicked off a series of 'people-power' revolutions around the world, and we don't care if we're recognized or not. And it was not a freak show, but one that's consistent with our history of inciting pocket rebellions.

The Philippines, for all its flaws, and there are far too many, does not have to hide such glistening skeletons in its closet. If at all, what we Filipinos have are watered-down versions. Yet despite everything, we never thought ourselves to be superior. In fact, we feel so inferior that we have to make such a long litany of insecurities like this. But this tragic sense of inferiority may yet prove to be our own salvation.

(This is a longer version of an article published in Fudge magazine, Jul. 2007)

15

The Precariousness of Being Pinoy

Resty Odon

Dateline, May 08, 2003

THE only constant in the universe, one Greek thinker said, is change. Change, however, does not fit the Filipino's definition of the universe. Uncertainty seems more appropriate. It has been the single driving force that pumps the nation's lifeblood such that the more things change, the more they remain the same. Uncertainty continues to define who and what we are. In its absence, life starts to feel funny and we turn uncharacteristically fidgety.

Bienvenido Santos (or was it someone else?) was really ahead of his time when he took to comparing the Pinoy to the bamboo. However, I am hesitant to extol our 'grassroots' resilience to the level of a virtue. For me, it's no more than a cultural trait conceived in the womb of uncertainty.

A paradoxical but palpable part of being Pinoy is the constant temptation to change one's nationality. It's a nightmare waking up one day to find your young nephews sporting a strange accent over the phone when they've been living in Canada for just a few months. A long time ago, I was astonished to find my father, who had been a contract worker in Saudi Arabia, naming our youngest brother Ibrahim. To my greater surprise, nobody objected to the name, not the least the baptizing priest who liked the Biblical ring to it.

Like bats that can't enter either the society of birds or beasts, Filipinos can neither be totally Asian nor Latino and certainly not Caucasians nor Africans. Nowhere is this cluelessness as glaring than in Philippine politics which I think should be patented for sheer inventiveness. Time and again, I would see this growing national idiosyncrasy and resilience against the backlash of fate. An intelligent president had proved us wrong so we resorted to, um, a more popular one. But show biz proved us wrong, too, so we're back to square one, another period of uncertainty which we are wont to celebrate—with another political circus.

The author of "The Beach" Alex Garland found something nice about this inconstancy, this uncertainty, calling the Philippines through his character Richard, "a democracy on paper, apparently well ordered, regularly subverted by irrational chaos..." Like Richard, we are at home with inconstancy, taking what should be surreal as matter-of fact.

And it's not just about government policies that constantly mutate with the change in administration. Our very archipelago sits on it. We are not situated on the Pacific Ring of Fire for nothing. Our islands straddle the crossroads of violent storms, including the storms of history. It's become an integral part of the Filipino psyche to contend with earthquakes, volcanic eruptions, typhoons, floods, economic downturns, coup d'etats and political chaos (i.e. elections).

Study our tongue and note how this tenor is carried through our day-today lingo. Observe the various permutations of our usual answers to absolute questions: Baka. Ewan. Malamang. Depende. Siguro. Sige. Oo, pero.. Tingnan natin. (Perhaps. I don't know. It depends. We'll see). Surely the matter is less about just being polite than simply being unsure?

Conservationist-architect Augusto Villalon has already noted this inconstancy in terms of architecture. The nipa hut is the quintessential Filipino architectural idiom. When we smash art deco treasures like the Metropolitan Theater with the wrecker's ball without the vaguest remorse, we are just being true to ourselves, inheritors of a peculiar past and children of the tropics through and through, where everything is rootless and rots fast, thanks to termites, a diverse array of fungi, the optimum humidity, and the most unruly, and thus corrosive, sociopolitical trade winds.

Pinoys are often accused of being a people without a soul but this is precisely our soul, one that thrives in the precariousness of existence. Wonder no more why we haven't produced anything great in the Western rubric of greatness. As perceptively noted by James Hamilton-Patterson in "The Ghost of Manila," we have no music to rival those of Bach and Beethoven, no epic that can stand shoulder to shoulder with Mahabharata, no structures like Angkor Wat or Borobudur, no handicraft to make the Burmese and the Thais envious. (Interestingly, E. M. Forster noted quite the same for England in "Howard's End" but England is altogether another species.)

Our greatness, which I think explains our much-touted resilience, lies in our total lack of illusion for permanence and eminence. Yes, dear structural conservationists, much as I hate it as well, there is wisdom in razing the Jai Alai fronton to the ground and it's not about the evil of gambling, either. Dear advocates of democracy, there is a trace of wisdom in Machiavellian politics and it's not about opportunism. And dear cineastes, there is wisdom in pito-pito (quickie) films and it's not merely about easy money.

The wisdom lies in either of two extremes: ingenuity and transcendence. "Things may never get better, so we might as well live life to the fullest, even under the worst circumstances." What is "a world-gone-berserk" to most people Filipinos call daily life; what is magical realism to Latinos, as one well-known writer puts it, we call documentary. Under such circumstances, one can only cling oh-so-tenaciously to life to survive. On the other hand, one cannot afford to stay too attached to life either. Interestingly bahala na (come what may)-- that quintessential throwaway Pinoy attitude in times of uncertainty-- straddles both extremes. Most see the first as vice and the second as virtue, so that both heaven and hell must be teeming with Filipinos. But think again: pragmatism is surely a virtue in the face of debilitating adversity while transcendence can easily be dismissed as escapism. No matter; this dualism is the successful art of coping, bearing fruit in the form of an indomitable spirit which would help us survive both poles and all latitudes of the globe. I figure that if the Earth veered off its spin and turned upside down, there's no second-guessing who would survive. After all, we've long been historically, geographically, tectonically in training, an anomalous phylum flourishing in an archipelago carelessly tattooed onto a sea of uncertainty. And, as already mentioned, if things suddenly go nice and easy, that's the time we turn really edgy. "Things can't possibly be this nice and easy; something must be wrong. It's simply not our life."

(Pub. in Sunday Inquirer Magazine on 1/14/01 , 2001)

16

Ode to My Alloy Nation

Resty Odon

Dateline, June 23, 2004

It's awful how people in authority define Filipino culture. I've noticed it as a pattern so glaringly wrong, this limitation of what is Filipino to things purely indigenous and think it to be a virtuous thing to do.

Maybe government and academia are right. I strongly suspect, however, that they're doing it as a face-saving measure in the face of James Fallow's (Atlantic Monthly) accusation of the Filipino as "a damaged culture." I find the response to be one that gives in anew to a foreign imposition of what is supposedly Filipino: one that's exotic in their eyes. It would certainly make Westerners happy in the touristy sense, but would it be truthful?

Pardon me, but what the heck is "truly Filipino"? It is like answering the question "What is truly American?" and answering it falsely with "Truly American means only Native Americans need apply."

That is offensive to me and it should be offensive to anyone in the world who's Filipino. It is a form of discrimination, albeit in the reverse sense, i.e., with the majority being discriminated against. Yes, the Ifugao mummy, the Maranao okir, the Aeta hunting dance, and the Hanunuo Mangyan's alibata variant are indeed Filipino, but why should we close our eyes on the contemporary realities of Philippine culture?

I have a friend whose mother is a college professor who often interacts with European academic types. He once recounted how, in a conference his mother attended in Scandinavia, his mother was surprised to discover that the Finns (or some other folks) would choose listening to the music of Yoyoy Villame if given the chance to choose among the existing types of modern Filipino music. "Ah, now this is truly Filipino!" they must have gushed.

That wouldn't be problematic except that they run the risk of being totally deceived. It's like saying Filipino culture is whatever the white man feels to be exotic. It is as though the Chinese, Spanish, American and even Japanese influences never came upon us. I mean, how many people listen to Yoyoy Villame as a daily pastime? How old is Filipino as a distinct cultural entity anyway to even merit comparison with such centuries-old cultures as the Thais, the Japanese, the Burmese, the Arabs, the Indians? We must remind ourselves that it was only after Rizal conceived of a Filipino nation that Filipinos became 'truly' Filipinos, and just how many decades back is that?

There is no denying that the alibata evolved to be entirely Filipino, but it is actually Indian plus some other in origin, but not a soul uses it for his day-to-day transaction. It's sad the tradition has been lost, but there is nothing wrong with the fact that even if we dig deeper anthropologically, we would be finding some other culture. The point is, that's what we are; we can never take pride in being "pure," if there is such a thing as cultural purity, because we are a wild amalgam trying to be a solid alloy. What culture hasn't borrowed something from some other anyway? Perhaps only those cultures most insular and insolently opinionated about themselves that they end up producing offspring with ostrich toes and hemophilic blood!

We have to live with the fact that the Filipino is a relatively young cultural entity, but that doesn't make it any less legitimate and any less vibrant than the rest of the world's cultures.

This is not to denigrate tribal arts and 'novelty acts' like Yoyoy Villame's music, either, but only putting them in their proper place, i.e., they are just a part in the vastly diverse panorama of things Philippine, and aren't we proud of that? Villame's lyrics, for one, has the wit and the good nature that's awfully missing in Joey de Leon and Lito Camo's tacky compositions. Having said that, no one seriously studying the Philippine music scene can say the local scene is dominated by Yoyoy Villame's songs. Nyoy Volante, Nina, Side A, The Eraserheads -- these are all Filipino, too. Yes, Filipino, not merely Western copycats, if we take a closer look.

And, so what, if these examples are, for want of a better term, Westernized? Does that make the Filipino inferior in the eyes of both the West and the East? More important, should that make us feel inferior about ourselves? The thing is, Filipino culture has a strong occidental face, and it is not just because of colonization, but because, as it is increasingly becoming evident to me, Filipinos only embrace what they like, the heck what others think about them, as though to say "This is who we are."

As a young, evolving cultural entity, Filipino-ness has become not a matter of saying "Hey, baby, I'm so proud to be colonized" but one of saying "These are the things I like, and I don't care what you think about it." I believe we have evolved from being an imposed-upon culture being forced-fed with something strange and unpalatable, to one that's trying to get rid of what it doesn't like, to one that has embraced what it thinks is essential and discarded what is chaff.

17

Precious Precariousness

Resty Odon

Dateline, November 05, 2006

In my three decades of existence, I've come to be comfortable with the precarious life. It's a state I've even come to embrace. I realized I've been operating from this different state of mind whenever I meet people who describe my life as one having no security, no clear direction, nothing.

I'm not exactly that live-for-the-moment guy who only aims to enjoy life in the epicurean sense. I'm coming from the roll-with-the-punches school, but not in the stoic sense, either.

Most people just don't get the difference between the two. It really takes a great adjustment in wavelengths for them to understand me, not that I am in the constant business of wanting to be understood.

I lost my full-time job four months ago, and it's not the lifetime-security kind of job to begin with. And yet I was even more at peace that I lost it. Finally. From normal people's viewpoint, I simply became unemployed. From my own vantage point, however, I was finally freed up from the usual corporate structures – the bundy clock, the performance evaluation matrix, down to the neatly pressed office uniform.

Once, in an MRT ride home, I got the jaw of my friend dropping to the floor when she learned that I have either cancelled or discontinued all of my existing insurance policies. While she clearly saw a non-husband material in me, I just kept quiet from the discovery of my 'humiliation' (Of course, I didn't look at it as such). I did not want to explain, although I admit I was kind of embarrassed that I was being pitied by someone I knew. I did not want to explain because she would not understand. I'm already having some trouble sorting things out for myself; need I have to explain myself to someone else as well?

The same thing happened over lunch with another friend. He actually mentioned the word precarious to describe my life situation, as though I was in ICU. And that made me laugh because it sounded true and yet ridiculous, at least to me. Who indeed will I run to when I get sick, meet a terrible accident, and get old all alone in the world without even a ghost to keep me company?

Sometimes people get me worrying about me needlessly. Thanks, but no thanks to them, I get visions of dying a bachelor trapped in my apartment and will not be discovered after 15 days – which is quite scary because it happens.

But, not to worry, they succeed only for a time. People get sick? Why, even people who never smoked a cigarette die of lung cancer. Please explain that to me. People die instantly in a car crash? Yes, they do, and all the money in the world can't save them. The problem with my no problem is people keep on reminding me that I have a big problem to solve, a terrible load upon my shoulder. No matter how good-intentioned, they never fail to convey their pity – and most likely, contempt – for me.

Often the immediate result is one of self-pity, a kind of self-realization that everybody else moved further up in the world and I was left in the pits. The next immediate result is envy: I want the same SUV, digicam, 3G phone, house and lot, love life, sex life, home life, prestigious address, master's degree, travels you have/have been doing!

A distant cousin called me up one day and, among other things, our exchange lapsed into the unspeakable. Out loud she mentioned she's alarmed as hell that I continue to give some of my meager income to other people. "Don't give too much," she advised from the goodness of her heart. "Think about yourself. Think about the time when you get old."

It was a profoundly caring advice, which I lap up dutifully for all its sweetness. But I am not the least bit deceived, or so I'd like to think. I pity these people more who pity me because they seem to have gotten it all, while I almost have nothing. I pity them because they got it all wrong.

They couldn't face up to the stark reality that there's no such thing as security, or certainty, in this world. Everything is an illusion when we miss focusing on the essentials that lie ahead.

But it could be that I am likewise deceiving myself. So I chose the right priorities. What then? What did I get out of it? Why did the supposed blessings not come? Why this, when I am actually in love, in lust, with the world, with the positive side of materialism, with all the excess, the art, the beauty life has to offer?

Well, let me sort this out first for myself. But I think the real question is why am I not being saddled by imponderable problems like I should? The thing is, I have this perverse enjoyment not many people share, I'm afraid; I actually enjoy my teetering position on the steep promontory of my day-to-day existence in this totally unpredictable, absolutely crazy city. I'm like that guy in the movie *As Good as It Gets*, who has this obsessive-compulsive behavior of avoiding all the cracks in the pavement; the difference is I find joy in stepping on anything that might give me that mixed feeling of falling down or sinking and keeping my head bobbing up.

As a so-called freelancer, I'm a circus act, delicately balancing myself between life and death, sickness and health, youth and old age, acceptance and rejection, peace and fear, happiness and sorrow, comfort and pain. I have long accepted that we can never change life for what it really is – precariousness itself, a constant battle at all fronts, with no predictable outcome. I have found that precariousness is something not to be feared but embraced and even celebrated. In planning my life, I'm half-Coveyan and half-... how do I put it... serendipitous. I'm open to both structure and amorphousness, certainty and unpredictability.

To be sure, I understand the importance of deceiving ourselves that the illusion is real, that things can be made constant, even eternal, even now. That is why for all its fancifulness, I neither appreciate nor like ephemeral art. I most assuredly lament the fact that it will be gone in a few seconds. But I still tend to take pictures of gorgeous sandcastles at the beach before they are lapped up by the sea. I want things I can freeze from my weak memory, framed for posterity. I believe staunchly in the conservation of species, in finding sustainable energy, and the preservation of material and intangible cultural heritage. In this regard, I would prefer van Gogh's "vanitas" series, which depicts this particular truth about precariousness but paradoxically preserves it in acrylic, on canvass.

The trouble with most people is they choose to be permanently deceived and they know it, i.e., until they forget that they've been had. By then, the delusion would have been complete, it threatens to be as irreversible as it is self-destructive.

I guess, unlike most people, I hate being lulled into this complacency, this nonchalance, that causes most of us to forget what's really essential. I refuse to be deceived that my friends will always be there, that my skin will continue to glow the next day, that I will wake up with all my hair intact tomorrow, that I will have my family with me through thick and thin, and so on. I believe people should experience being betrayed by their closest allies, one day losing their job, seeing a cohesive social group splitting into factions, witnessing an entire society crumbling in disarray, etc., to understand where I'm coming from. I'm not advocating the celebration of the ugly, nor am I championing disorder. I only advise that people be aware of the constancy of inconstancy and be consistently wary of feeling so smug about their vision of the future and so called security.

I want to believe there should be an awareness that all of human civilization is but a grand delusion, in a way. We should all be reminded how and when the end of it all shall come – in medias res, like Aristotle would have put it, "in the midst of it all," when people are marrying and are being given up for marriage, when people make merriment without a thought for the morrow, and so on. I only ask that we be cognizant of the frailty of our faculties, keen on the knowledge that we can lose it all even just when we begin to enjoy it. I know people tend not to listen. Well, they're just being consistent with being people. But I argue for that point just the same. If they still don't listen, then I keep quiet. I have said my piece, what's needed to be uttered, and now I deserve to leave and retire in peace, in the embrace of the here and now, planned on a day-to-day basis.

I wish I could convince everyone that it is when we give everything up – especially our attachment for our personal and professional achievements - our very notion of worldly success, peace and security, and identity - will we achieve a keener enjoyment of life in its fullness. It is when we give up everything and stay detached that we will achieve true success, peace, security, identity, achievement. It's more a wishful thinking on my part, I know, but I have to do my part of not giving up just the same. If am not listened to, it shall not be my loss.

If I have a big problem with the concept of security, it's because, when you think about it, it's the rat race in the name of so-called security that makes us and the world all the poorer for it. This is exactly what marginalizes a lot of people. The kind of notion of security that causes us to miss out on a lot of wonderful gifts, to paraphrase a line from a talk I once attended.

Let us take a brief look at American imperialism for the apotheosis of this universal mindset. When America encroached on 'Injun' country and claimed the Native Americans as their own, and when Americans enslaved blacks from Africa and claimed them as their property (actually they were only following European traditions.), -- all in the name of peace and security, of course –

Americans became all the poorer, all the more politically unstable and precarious for it. It was only when the white supremacists freed up their slaves did the gifted musicality and Olympic-caliber stamina and sportsmanship of black people emerged and America got all the richer for it. What is true for the American story is true for our own respective domestic stories. Life rewards us over-abundantly when we embrace the beauty that lies in precariousness.

18

Heart to Heart -
Violence On Television, Etc

Philip S. Chua, MD, FACS, FPCS

(All articles by Dr. Chua. Printed with permission from the author of the book Let's Stop 'Killing' Our Children by Philip S. Chua, MD, FACS, FPCS, published by Xlibris, August 2011.)

The cultures of corruption and of violence in society are close cousins, if not twins. They are intertwined. Where there is corruption, there is violence, and vice versa. Violence is a symptom of a corrupt mind, and corruption is violence against fellow human beings and society.

Are we more violent as a society today? Do video games subliminally brain-wash our young children's mind as they take pleasure in actively participating in virtual massive killings as an accepted form of entertainment? Do these violent games make these kids take violence and killings, and the Ten Commandments, more lightly?

Studies have shown that watching educational and socially interactive children's shows on television have positive impacts on these children, not only in learning arithmetic or science but in social behavior, humanity, compassion, honesty and responsibility.

On the other end of the spectrum, young boys and girls alike, who watch violence on television have increased risk of aggression, including spousal abuse and criminal offenses as adults. Violence on any media adversely affects children's lives by eroding into their inborn and natural aversion to violence, making aggression, violence, and in many cases, crime as acceptable social behaviors for them when dealing with their family and the public.

Adults are not immune to these negative effects. Most of us have heard the "F" word mentioned so many times in one sentence in western shows and simply laugh at it. Some of us Filipinos, including women, have even acquired this cursing habit too casually, although some mispronounce the letter "F," making it doubly embarrassing.

Children learn from what they see and what they hear, at home or in their world outside. They grow up with all those experiences, and they become the summation of what they learn. Whichever predominates rule their future.

W, as parents, have the grave responsibility of protecting our children from any form of harm, including negative influences, and of guiding them to become good, law-abiding, honest, productive, and compassionate citizens, making them a credit to society and to the human race as a whole.

Drinking and Blood Pressure

Mix binge drinking and high blood pressure and you get a cocktail of medical conditions that shortens longevity. Indeed, binge drinking among those with hypertension increases the risk of death, compared to those persons with normal blood pressure. A lot of alcohol and high blood pressure are a lethal mix.

Binge drinking, which is a major public health issue, is defined as consuming a large amount of alcoholic drink in one single session. While it is a serious health problem, many drinkers are ignorant of the risks. Alcohol poisoning from binge drinking is not rare.

Published in STROKE: Journal of the American Heart Association, the South Korean study involving 6,100 subjects over twenty years found that "compared to people with normal blood pressure who did not drink, the risk of cardiovascular death in men, with high blood pressure was 3 times higher in general; 4 times higher if they consumed at least 6 drinks in one binge session; 12 times higher if they consumed at least 12 drinks in one binge session."

The American Heart Association defines moderate drinking as "a maximum of two drinks per day for men and one drink per day for women...a drink is defined as a 12-ounce beer, one 4-ounce glass of wine, 1.5 ounces of 80-proof spirits or one ounce of 100-proof spirits."

When gambling hurts

Gambling as an entertainment has been with us even before civilization started. Cavemen had their own version of gambling. Casinos have spread all over the United States, a few in the Philippines, many in Macao, Monaco, and other countries. Today, we even have online gambling, internet betting, using credit cards to purchase chips.

Gambling at home (mahjong, poker, blackjack, bingo, etc.) for charity or not, or gambling in casinos, for fun, with discipline and limitations in terms of amount and time, can be refreshing, especially with friends. But uncontrolled frequent gambling, even at home with friends, especially with high stakes (no longer penny-ante friendly wager), is addictive gambling no less.

When one is helplessly hooked on gambling, a so-called "hidden illness," which the sufferer may not even realize, or has self-denial about it, or actually covering it up because of shame, then the fun has long stopped, and the stage of addiction has set in. Many obsessive gamblers are also alcoholics, where weakness in the character appears to play a role, according to psychotherapists.

The strong uncontrollable urge to gamble dominates the victim, up to the point of giving up food, sleep, personal grooming, his job, his social life, and neglecting his family, in favor of gambling. Since habitual gambling is a losing game and a game of losers, soon the victim parts with all his money, his property, his self-respect, his friends, even his family. As the stress escalates, he resorts to more gambling in his desire to chase (win back) his loses. So, he goes deeper and deeper, in financial and emotional bankruptcy. Not a few of them ended up killing themselves, like a couple of physicians I have heard of.

Some of the signs and symptoms include changes of personality, attention, and responsibility; losing time from work or school; borrowing money or pawning or selling personal possessions; lying about amount and time wasted on gambling; gambling to escape problems; and having a sense of fear, depression, frustration, anger, hopelessness, and suicidal tendencies.

Addictive gambling is a disease, and like other illnesses, it could benefit from early attention, diagnosis, and prompt treatment. There are centers and support groups, which can help. Taking this wise and prudent step towards healing is one gamble the victim can bet on with his life, and usually win big!

19

Heart to Heart - Attitude Impacts Health, Life

Philip S. Chua, MD, FACS, FPCS

Show me a man with an attitude and I will show you one abandoned by his friends and scorned by strangers he irritated and riled.

Here are some quotes of wisdom I have come across which are inspiring philosophical parachutes in life for those who, like many of us, sometimes find themselves falling towards the pit of discouragement and despair. With the proper attitude, these sage proverbs lift our spirit by allowing us to view and accept the trials and tribulations in this world in their most positive and best light. Indeed, all of us need a psychological boost, an inspiration, every now and then. Here are some:

Anthony J. D'Angelo, in The College Blue Book, said "Wherever you go, no matter what the weather, always bring your own sunshine." To quote Oscar Wilde, "If you don't get everything you want, think of the things you don't get that you don't want."

Voltaire expressed it beautifully when he stated, "Life is like a shipwreck, but we must not forget to sing in the lifeboats." An ancient Persian saying puts a great perspective on our daily aches and pains in life, "I had the blues because I had no shoes until upon the street, I met a man who had no feet." And as some of us may curse some bad days we encounter and wish they never came. Cavett Robert offers these poignant words: "If you don't think every day is a good day, just try missing one."

Indeed, every day is a good day, although others are better, and others not as good. But each day is a gift. Not waking up to another day is a deadly waste, but not appreciating another day as we open our eyes each morning in our journey through life is a tragedy. How each of us greets the day depends greatly on our attitude. Indeed, attitude impacts our health, our life, and our everyday happiness and success. A person with a chip on his shoulder, with a negative attitude or pessimistic view of life, will obviously be miserable most of the time. And the opposite is true, as Annette Goodheart brilliantly points out: "Just because you're miserable doesn't mean you can't enjoy life."

Happiness is basically an attitude. Gaining inner peace is an attitude. We have that God-given power to feel what we want to feel. And we can even psyche ourselves. I do.

When I wake up each morning, I thank God for another wonderful day. And I tell my mind ahead of time that it will be another good day. It may not be a perfect day, but a good, pleasurable and productive one, a day I could enjoy being with my family, doing my computer works, writing my column to help inform, educate and entertain people, challenging our fellowmen to open their heart to Gawad Kalinga to help our poor fellowmen languishing in abject poverty in the Philippines and around the world, promoting the moral crusade of the Filipino United Network (USA) and other advocacy groups in our campaign for good governance in our home country, or to simply complement someone, inspire somebody, do open heart surgery, or just touch a heart, plant a tree, and enjoy the sunset and the beauty of the universe.

In a world where global peace is still a dream, a world beset with an economic crisis, with terrorism, with greed and corruption, with energy, food and water shortage, global warming and its devastating side-effects or typhoons, earthquakes and flooding, a good attitude, in the midst of all these disasters, is one of our best weapons against helplessness, despair and depression.

With all these complex problems confronting us, we often find ourselves in the gutter of hopelessness, wherefrom, Oscar Wilde suggests, we can look up at the heavens and "see the stars." Indeed, a positive attitude, a happy outlook in life, especially these days, can help us tremendously in conquering our fears, insecurities, and dilemmas. Without total surrender, when we sometimes lose or fail, we should remind ourselves to get up and fight even harder. After all, "defeat is not bitter unless you swallow it," as Joe Clark states. To this, I will add my own: "No one can succeed in life who does not have the courage to fail"; and, "The greatest risk in life is in not taking any risk at all."

Someone said, "You cannot adjust the direction of the wind, but you can adjust your sail." Very true, indeed. Simple words of wisdom that could make our day, if not our life.

And all this leads me to quote a very popular soothing prayer that you may know, one that I say almost every day of my life, immediately following the expression of my thanks to the Almighty: "God, grant me the

Serenity to accept the things I cannot change; Courage to change the things I can; and the Wisdom to know the difference."

My faith in God, my acceptance and submission to His will, eliminates more than 75% of my worries day in and day out. I do not dwell on things I cannot change and allow fear and despair to paralyze my life. Worrying about things outside of my control is a waste of my time and expensive emotion that takes a toll on my mental and physical health. The things beyond my power I leave to God, and in doing so, I free my mind of a lot of unhealthy baggage.

But, of course, we should not simply leave everything to God. We must do our share. He promises to help those who help themselves. While we cannot cure the cancer of poverty in our country, we, as individuals, who are more blessed, can at least open our heart to help the homeless and the hungry, and gain that sense of satisfaction and inner peace. As I have stated a few times in the past, let us not wait for surgery to open our heart. Let our good attitude and compassion for our fellowmen reign.

As I live my life each day, I remind myself of an ancient proverb that says, "To everyone is given the key to heaven; the same key opens the gates to hell." It's indeed a matter of personal choice. And that choice inevitably depends on our attitude in life. Some people believe their fate is predestined, and that they can't do anything about it. Others, inspired by good attitude and a positive frame of mind, design, create, and charter their own destiny.

Finally, I strongly believe that leaving this world after this life is not a tragedy. Dying without significance, without making a difference, without leaving behind a good legacy, is.

Let's all develop a good attitude to help us enjoy life. It's a potent prescription for health and happiness.

20

Heart to Heart - Are We Getting Enough Sleep?

With Philip S. Chua, MD, FACS, FPCS

"Most American adults sleep poorly," according to a study of the National Sleep Foundation on 1506 adults which was reported in Washington by the Associated Press. The findings are obviously applicable to most of us in general.

Lack of sleep translates to lesser mental acuity and concentration, poorer health, greater driving hazards, reduced productivity, and diminished sex drive.

Sleep experts recommend a minimum of 7 to 9 hours of sleep in 24 hours.
The survey showed that adults sleep an average of 6.9 hours a night. The few minutes to 3 hours of sleep deprivation is enough to cause problems.

Seventy-five percent of adults reported they frequently have difficulty in sleeping, like problem in initiating sleep, waking up often during the night, and/or snoring, waking up too early, and feeling unrefreshed and tired. Many also stated that they ignored the problem, and some do not even think they actually have any sleep deficit. Only about 50% of those surveyed stated they were able to sleep well most of the time. Twenty five percent thought their sleep problem had adverse effects on their daily routines.

Richard Gelula, the Chief Executive Officer of the Sleep Foundation, said there's a link between sleep and quality of life. "People who sleep well, in general, are happier and healthier," said Gelula. "But when sleep is poor or inadequate, people feel tired or fatigued, their social and intimate relationship suffer, work productivity is negatively affected, and they make our roads more dangerous by driving while sleepy and less alert."

Obviously, the quality of sleep, besides the number of hours, is very important. Chris Drake, senior scientist at the Henry Ford Sleep Center in Detroit and co-chair of the 2005 poll task force, stated that some of the nation's sleep habits can be attributed to an "always-on-the-go society."

The commercial world of today stretches business to 24 hours a day, with 24-hour pharmacy, restaurants, casinos, supermarkets, etc., so people tend to stay up late, watch late night shows on television, surfing the web on the internet, etc. All these reduce people's time to sleep. And some people even need more than 9 hours of sleep to feel refreshed and rested.

This study also showed (1) Sixty percent of adult stated they have driven a vehicle while drowsy from lack of sleep the past year; and 4 in 10 reported they have had an accident or near accident because of tiredness or falling asleep at the wheel. (2) Seventy five percent claims their partner has a sleep problem, snoring as the most common complaint. (3) Four out of ten of those surveyed reported lack of sleep adversely affected their sexual relationship, having lost interest in sex, having poorer performance or having sex less often. (4) Seventy percent claimed that their physician never asked them about their sleep.

The recommendations of the National Sleep Foundation and experts in the field are abstinence from any stimulant, coffee and alcohol before bedtime, and to seek medical help if they think they are having sleep problem and/or snoring, or not getting enough rest at night.

Lack of sleep reduces the normal "recharging time of our body battery, our energy source" causing a chain of reactions in our physiology and body chemistry. This "lo-bat" condition leads to physical and mental stresses to our system. All these alter the normal homeostasis (internal balance) within us, weakening our immune system, and increasing our risk of developing metabolic diseases, hypertension (high blood pressure), stroke and heart attack, among others, or aggravating existing illnesses.

The prescription for a healthy lifestyle, for maximal maintenance of good health and disease prevention, besides regular medical check-up, includes the following ingredients: Adequate sleep, rest and relaxation, total abstinence from tobacco, strict moderation in alcohol intake (a glass or two of red wine with dinner is great), daily exercises (like brisk walking), low-fat, low-cholesterol, low-carb, high-fiber diet (vegetables, fruits, grains, nuts, etc), and, equally important, having a happy and positive attitude in life.

21

Heart to Heart - Obesity: A Killer

Philip S. Chua, MD, FACS, FPCS

Look anywhere, or better yet, go to a hamburger restaurant or a junk food store, and you will surely see children who are overweight, if not obese, a growing time-bomb, clicking and soon ready to explode. Many times, both of the parents and the other siblings are also overweight. Statistically, one in three children and adolescents is overweight, even higher in some minority segment of society.

Indeed, there is an obesity epidemic around us, more appropriately, a pandemic, since this unfortunate situation is happening all over the world, except perhaps in Africa and other third world countries where famine is the other extreme that is killing children prematurely. This pandemic started in the 1970s, when society was not weight-conscious and the unpopular medical warnings were simply ignored. As a result, today we have a third of the children population of the world who have fallen victims to a potentially deadly condition called childhood obesity.

But what's wrong with a cute plump overweight child? The child might be a gorgeous and "healthy-looking" kid, but medically, the youngster's condition is a disaster waiting happen. As countless studies have shown repeatedly, the prognosis for this beautiful young life with excess weight is dismal compared to children with normal weight. The same scientific findings are true with adults, everything else being equal. And it affects not only health but longevity.

The topic of diseases and lifestyle always reminds me of two past personal experiences in my life. The first one is the premature demise of my Dad, who was overweight, a heavy smoker, sedentary, and a hypertensive (high blood pressure), who succumbed to a heart attack at age 46 in 1962. My mother is 93, still doing video exercise every morning. My father would still be alive today, if the physicians then had the advanced knowledge and technology, like what we have today. At that time, even the cardiologist did not know that simple aspirin could help thin the blood and minimize heart attack. We did not have cardiac cath and angiogram then, much less, angioplasty and heart bypass surgery.

The second was the time when I performed triple coronary bypass surgery in the early 90s on a 28-year-old overweight lady, who, at that young age, was most unhealthy --- a chronic cigarette-smoker, a diabetic, with hypertension and elevated cholesterol and triglyceride blood levels. Feeling well after surgery, she resumed her old bad habits of smoking, diet of red meats and eggs, and no exercise. The unhealthy lifestyle brought her back on the operating table 5 years after the first surgery. She has since behaved and leading a healthier and more productive life. The fundamental question is, what impact will the her bad medical history (caused by her past unhealthy habits) have in her longevity?

The case of this patient is not uncommon. Heart patients are getting younger and younger. And obesity is one of the major causes of asthma, depression, acid reflux, hypertension, hyperlipidemia (high cholesterol/lipids), heart disease, diabetes, stroke, and even cancer. Two new studies published in the New England Journal of Medicine predicts "a significant increase in the number of potentially fatal coronary heart disease cases in adults over the next few decades as a result of the prevalence of overweight kids today."

Investigators at the University of California, San Francisco, "using current childhood obesity figures, historical trend data and scientific models, project in one study that by 2035 the prevalence of coronary heart disease in the United States will increase as much as 16 percent, with more than 100,000 excess cases of the disease attributable to the rise in obesity among kids."

A separate study conducted by Danish researchers, "used health data from 276,835 Danes, as they grew from schoolchildren into adults, and found that those with a higher body mass index (a measure of body fat based on height and weight) in childhood had an increased risk of developing heart disease as adults."

Dr. David Ludwig, director of the Optimal Weight for Life Program at Children's Hospital Boston and an associate professor of pediatrics at Harvard Medical School, warns that "without intervention the costs of childhood obesity may well become catastrophic," a fact he stressed in an interview with Newsweek's Jennifer Barrett.

If not controlled early in life, obesity becomes permanent, and the bad effects of obesity on the body physiology stay throughout the adult life of the individual. A significant of number of youngsters with type 2 diabetes were cured with diet and weight control alone, others, with pills on top of weight management. This proves how normal weight can protect the body and its functions, including the immune system.

Carbohydrates (rice, bread, sugar, cakes, ice cream, candies, most sweets, non-diet soft drinks, other junk foods, etc) are a major culprit in weight gain and obesity in children and in adults. Since carbohydrates are also found in fish, vegetables, fruits, nuts and grains (the healthy food items), those carbo items listed above are not really necessary in our diet. Staying away from carbo (especially rice, sweets, and pop drinks) will amazingly help in weight control faster than you can imagine. So carbo and fats are out and healthy protein is in, including bean curd (tofu) and other soya products.

Let's all help stop this catastrophe-in-the-making in our own home. As I have suggested in previous articles, we, parents, must learn how to say "no" to our children, discipline them early to live a healthy lifestyle, and to stop "killing" them in the name of love.

22

Are We The Disappearing Breed of Professionals in this Country?

Dr. Caesar D. Candari, MD, FCAP EMERITUS

(The author is   A Dynamic Leader and A Perfect Role Model. Appointed as the first Filipino Commissioner of the Governing Board of San Diego Stadium Authority, and as a Field Commissioner of the Licensing Division of the State Medical Board of California, Dr. Candari concretely exemplifies the multi-talents contribution of the Filipino-Americans to mainstream-America. **Cesar D. Candari**, *M.D., FCAP Emeritus, is a retired pathologist of Mercy Hospital and Medical Center (now Mercy Scripps), San Diego for 30 years. He is Diplomate in Anatomic and Clinical Pathology, and the first Filipino-American pathologist who was Certified Specialist in Blood Banking. He is a high school valedictorian. He graduated from the Far Eastern University, Institute of Medicine, Manila Philippines in 1961. He was one of the three Filipino American doctors who founded Operation Samahan Community Health Clinic and volunteered for 17 years mostly as chairman of the board. He held several major positions in the medical and specialty organizations. As editorial contributor for Filipino Press Newspaper in San Diego for several years, his journalistic style is written in simple and straightforward manner. He just wrote a book,* **"Success Is A Jouney"** *under Tatay Jobo Elizes Publishing.)*

(FROM ANTIQUE TO AMERICA: Memoirs of a Filipino American Doctor)

The changes in immigration policies in this country as we have seen have indeed harmed the continued influx of professionals, doctors, lawyers, engineers, nurses, and others. The previous fifth preference category, others, has virtually disappeared. Why is that? Reality check says it is the fear of competition, the economic competition imposed by the professional immigrants. Now as we grow older and finally retire questions are being raised. Who is going to follow our footsteps? Are we the disappearing breed of professionals in this country?

As of now, it is believe there is no shortage of physicians in the U.S. However, there are some states that expect shortage in physicians in year 2020 and those Filipino doctors who became nurses with working visas, and with no immigrant visas that are available right now, maybe they shall have a chance to become doctors again. Another visa available is the J-1 Visa in all states where there are medically underserved areas or health professional shortage areas.

Those physicians in the temporary worker visa or H-1B, is an alternative to J-1 visa, which is a two-year residency program in the U.S. In order to obtain the H-1B status, the physician must pass all parts of either the FLEX, the NBME, or the USMLE examinations. Upon completion of their residency programs, these physicians are able to obtain H-1B visas and permanent resident status through employer sponsorship. Others are able to immigrate to the U.S. through close relatives who are U.S. citizens or permanent residents. To Filipino doctors who are seeking employment in the US should bear in mind that there are special licensing requirements, and because of this they must start planning before the completion of medical school. Getting an H-1B visa is not always easy and even getting H-1B status is not free from problems. For further assistance, consult your immigration lawyers.

About seven decades ago, the Philippines gained its independence from the United States of America. This was a product of our natural quest for democracy and freedom. No one, I suppose, ever dreamt that thirty to forty years later or so, after that Independence Day, that you and I shall be here in America enjoying the freedom of this beautiful country and be blessed with opportunities and achieved success and affluence in our lives. We are indeed very fortunate if we compare ourselves with our colleagues in the Philippines, who are still yearning to come to America.

We all came to this country from all walks of life, of different professions, and with different perspectives and ambitions. We have struggled. Many of us have won in our struggles with flying colors, even exceeding our American counterparts. The rewards have been numerous. However, let us not be trapped into a state of complacency simply because we are doing well. There will always be challenges out there. There is no doubt that the contribution of the Foreign Medical Graduates and the Foreign Nursing Graduates in the health system of this country is substantial. Let no one disregard this.

I truly believe we must concern ourselves to helping our country, and even more to our unfortunate colleagues who can never find decent careers in the Philippines.

While we concern ourselves in helping our countrymen and their ills, we must also develop our Filipino American community in its political clout in this country if we are to be effective in fighting oppressive and adverse policies. There is much to be done if we intend to forge our Filipino American community into a strong, cohesive force that can speak with one voice on matters that concern us all.

For Filipino nurses: With the worldwide aspiration to go to the US competing at each other, we can only imagine that the backlog (retrogression) of US Visa will continue to be a major hindrance for many Filipinos to go to the States. The only real hope in the horizon is the passing of the US Emergency Nursing Supply Release Act of 2008 or HR 5924.

The retrogression continues to be the reasons why no visas for competent nurses applying for work in the US are available, thus resulting to delay in their employment overseas.

The retirement of registered nurses (RNs), compounded by the increasing demand for health care services account for the large vacuum in such shortage.

As an organized grouped of Filipino American doctors and Filipino American nurses, we have a purpose for being. That purpose is no less than to help assure our survival as medical and nursing practitioners, as respectable human beings, to be given the opportunity without bias, to flourish and to achieve our maximum potential. The Philippine Nurses Association could make representations directly to the American Nursing Association and express their views and concerns. This is why it is very important to take active roles in our local, state, and national organization. Let us be recognized and our voices heard. Therefore, I urge each and every one of you to be active in your association. We in the community should dismiss all reservations concerning the capabilities of our associations. We must resolve our past and current jealousies and conflicts among the members of the community and overcome the apathetic Filipino syndrome to rise in the American mainstream by any means.

Finally, I'd like to share with you this consoling note: even if restrictions for our professions to enter as immigrants to this country are now behind us, we now have a second generation of Filipino Americans who are in college, nursing and medical schools, they will carry our heritage of which we have preserved. If we instill in our children and in our grandchildren the treasured tradition of our culture, they will always be proud as Filipinos. If we share with our children and our grandchildren the rewards and satisfaction of being in our profession, we will be encouraging them to follow in our footsteps. In this manner, there will always be a continuing supply of Fil-Am doctors and nurses in the U.S. to preserve our traditions and ideals. This scenario, if accomplished, will be a great day, and you and I can be very happy and proud of our organizations continuing in perpetuity.

23

If You Dream It, Do It Retirement

CESAR D. CANDARI, M.D., FCAP EMERITUS

As of this writing, volumes of articles about early retirement of doctors are now available. When the medical overhaul plan was under consideration by President Obama, two of every three practicing physicians opposed, and hundreds of thousands had the intentions of shutting down their practices or retiring early if it were adopted.

It was a poll by Investor's Business Daily (IBD) and TechnoMetrica Market Intelligence (TIPP) that four of nine doctors, or 45%, said they "would consider leaving their practice or taking an early retirement" if Congress passes the plan the Democratic majority and White House have in mind. More than 800,000 doctors were practicing in 2006, the government says. Projecting the poll's finding onto that population, 360,000 doctors would consider quitting. The poll contradicts the claims of not only the White House, but also doctors' own lobby — the powerful American Medical Association — both of which suggest the medical profession is behind the proposed overhaul. Two thirds, or 65%, of doctors say they oppose the proposed government expansion plan. Nowhere in the story does it say doctors as a whole back the overhaul. It says only that the AMA — the "association representing the nation's physicians" and what "many still regard as the country's premier lobbying force" — is "lobbying and advertising to win public support for President Obama's sweeping plan." Do you know that the AMA, in fact, represents approximately 18% of physicians only and has been hit with a number of defections by members opposed to the AMA's support of Democrats' proposed health care overhaul.

Now we know what happened. Health care reform in the United States in 2010 was enacted nationally.

The Filipino-American doctors might be a part of this 360,000 considering quitting or retiring early. While you are both still in the prime of life, you look forward to this momentous milestone, your retirement, as the next adventure in your lives to pursue the finer aspects of life, family and community as you put the troubles and pressures of the medical profession behind you.

After devoting so many years of your life in working, you will soon be able to devote more of your time to the interest, which you enjoy including service to the Philippine community and ongoing medical missions for the poor in the Philippines and around the world. Although you will be retired from your work, you will not be retired from the good things in life.

I have written articles about early retirement that was published in the APPA quarterly magazine back in 1988 and 1989. These dates were about ten years before I decided to retire. Therefore, I spent about a decade to plan my early retirement, as it was my dream. As the theme of my burning desire is about dreams, aspiration and goals, I never stopped reaching my hands to that untouchable star.

All in all the practice of medicine does not offer personal fulfillment anymore, but instead is fraught with tension and pressure. Many have said that they will never retire;

nonetheless, the stress of work, Medicare and malpractice threat will eventually make them realize that enough is enough. Consequently, you should get ready, whether you like it or not and plan for that retirement. In addition to having a retirement timetable, you must also know where to spend it enjoyably.

A good number of doctors are afraid to retire at an earlier age because they think they will have nothing to do. They are worried of boredom and that friends have told them that they will go crazy and die early. For as long as the pension pay off is adequate and they do not have to face a lot of adjustments, things will go smoothly. The good question is when will they enjoy that money?

Now is the time to spend it on living the life you like. Many of you have been blessed and are contented in this great country. You worked hard to earn a living and no doubt, achieved success and affluence in your lives one way or another. It is probably correct to say that you and your spouse have worked continuously for the last thirty years and some may be working towards your second retirement. Now, as the job begins to wear you down, it is time to enjoy life and start making plans for your retirement. Although to some this may be a premature question, planning ahead is never wrong.

Have you planned what you will do when you retire? To some it is a dreadful situation to think about. However, to others, they could not wait and are eagerly looking forward to it.

In these times of economic uncertainty, inflation, recession and energy crisis, planning for tomorrow is an extremely tricky business. The shrinking dollar is the number one problem facing anyone trying to guarantee himself a comfortable retirement in this country. Therefore there has to be an alternative to a "better life", and it should not be difficult for most Filipino-Americans doctors to achieve it upon retirement. That alternative is the Philippines. The biggest allure that living in the Philippines can offer is money value.

For one thing, the cost-of-living in the Philippines is very advantageous for someone earning a pension in U.S. dollars.

Here is one retirement plan that you might consider. Have you thought of spending your retirement time in Manila, Philippines? Do you realize that Manila speaks the merriest version of things that it can offer to individuals with reasonable retirement income? Think of the things you have been putting off for 20 years of working, like golf, tennis, travel, fishing, and comfortable living. How about going back home to your hometown you loved? Aside from being home with your friends and relatives, you have accomplished that burning desire of returning home. Plan something of establishing a home with all the amenities you can afford and enjoy. If you chose to stay in Manila, you may contribute to the advancement of medical standards in our country, be it in direct participation with the Post Graduate Medical Training Program in the Philippines, the recreational and cultural amenities and outlets for your personal interests are all there. For one thing, you are at the prime of your of your life, very active and functioning both mentally and physically. You accomplish your wishes and desire to help your countrymen; you will have emotionally satisfying and very comfortable living conditions. This is not to say that you will retire for good in the Philippines.I have been informed that Tagaytay City is an ideal retirement location. It has a marvelous mild tropical climate. An attractive secured gated community with linkages to adjoining towns and provinces are the blueprint at your disposal, you will have a butler, house help, a gardener, and a driver all of these at a cost you can easily afford. There will be extra cash to invest in any of your favorite charitable projects or other business opportunities that may employ your town mates, friends and relatives. It will have a lot of spare time. Therefore, realistically at an earlier age, you can retire and enjoy it all. If you dream it, do it !

24

Only In America - Human Interest Story

Anonymous

(The author chose to remain anonymous but he is my close friend. Thanks)

Every person has the freedom to observe and define the world for himself the way he sees it. A friend uses phrases like "born to serve" "not capable" "ordered and servant to a White Man." but is that the truth? No, it is not. Does it matter to me if my friend speaks the truth or not? No, it does not. What he says will not affect my life one way or another in the least. He can revel in his own ignorance.

I am a product of the free public school education established by the Americans. I attended the regular Elementary and High School in Manila, Philippines. I finished my Architect Degree at the prestigious University of the Philippines.

I grew up in Trozo, a middle-class district of Manila where Emilio Jacinto was born and where Rizal's family lived after his execution. After WWII, refugees from the provinces settled in Trozo in slum shacks along the estero de palomar. When jobs were available they worked as manual laborers. When jobs were not available they turned to crime to support their families. They were good people who were not fortunate enough to get an education. Their children were my friends. We went to the same free public elementary and high schools.

My father was an architect. I followed his footsteps. After graduation, he was appointed by the Director of public works, who was also his professor at Mapua Tech, to be the resident Architect of the Jai-Alai bldg, to work with an american architect there. Very early in his career he was stricken with asthma which troubled him for the rest of his life, succumbing to it at the age of 59. My mother was a Home Economics teacher, teaching elementary-school children. after the war, in the early 1950s when my father could not work anymore my mother worked as a city hall clerk to support their 7 children. When there was not enough money to send all of them to school, she borrowed money from relatives and friends to get us through. they knew that without an education, we would be disadvantaged in our adult lives. I am thankful to the Americans for founding the UP and allowing me to get a university education.

I left Manila in 1965, at the age of 24, to try my luck in America. Two of my friends from our employer-engineering-company in Philippines had left months earlier and were working for a New Haven, CT firm. I arrived in America on a friday and was at work with them the following Monday, trying hard not to fall asleep from jet lag. We were respected by our bosses and co-workers. A few of them were GIs who fought in the philippines and regaled us with war stories. One of the them was an airborne paratrooper who jumped into Tagaytay Ridge. Another was a seabee (CB-construction battalion) who helped clear the Leyte beaches so Macarthur could land and have his famous picture taken. They had fond memories of the Philippines and welcomed us with open arms as brothers.

With our american-style UP education we fit right in and tackled any work our bosses gave us. One boss called us the whiz kids because we could do everything he gave us and do it fast. He showed us a picture and the letters of a young Filipina child in a province he was sending $15 to every month to support her education. He was a first-generation Italian-American who told us of the discrimination he went through growing up. He treated us filipinos like his own family. He invited us to their huge italian family gatherings. i gave him a record of conching rosal's kundimans and after listening to them he told us we stole their music! he told my wife her meatloaf we served tastes just like the way his mother made it. we served them morcon and later his wife made us the italian braciola which was similar to it. Little things like that in my life convinced me that we human beings are all alike. Without our geopolitical labels attached to us we are the same people with the same needs and desires in life.

Later on in my career I became a VP of an alexandria, VA firm. I was a project manager in charge of my own projects with a staff to assist me. They were British-Americans, Irish-Americans, Scottish-Americans, Turkish-Americans, German-Americans, Polish-Americans, Cuban-Americans, Korean-Americans, Filipino-Americans, African-Americans, Portuguese-Americans, Colombian-Americans, who themselves or their forebears came from another country from another part of the world and ended up in America. My boss, the Company President, was a first-generation German-American, whose parents immigrated to Mankato, MN. He told me his immigrant parents were scared of what the other Americans would do to them during WWII. H was like an older brother to me. We still wish each other a happy birthday without fail every year.

America is an equal-opportunity country. One advances through merit. As anything in life, one can find exceptions to that rule. I had a young, black, high-school educated draftsman whose life still inspires me today. I am very proud of what he has made of himself. He is what america is all about. I would like to share his amazing life story with you:

"In 1972, after working there for 7 years, I moved from Connecticut to Virginia to work for another architectural-engineering company. There I met a teenaged black youth, recently graduated from high school. He was a very enthusiastic, handsome, friendly, hard-working, all-smiles kind of a guy. He was the company gofer - he ran errands for everyone in the company - he was the print boy, he replaced burned-out bulbs, made and served coffee to the bosses, ran out for their sandwiches at lunch, the courier who hand-delivered documents to other firms and company clients and washed the company cars. He showed dedication and love for his work. It seemed that he enjoyed whatever he was asked to do. He was unlike most menial workers who hated their jobs and the people who lorded over them. He was always ready to do anyone in the office a favor when asked, and always he flashed his engaging smile.

During his free times, between errands, he loved to sit down and learn drafting. He would take a pencil and with the T-square and triangles he would copy the plans and details of the project working drawings lying around. He would ask the draftsmen sitting next to him what the symbols represented. He was a dry sponge ready to absorb everything he could learn.

It soon became apparent to everyone over time that he had acquired the basic skills of a trained draftsman. Little by little he would be asked to help on the projects to meet deadlines. I grew to admire and respect his abilities and talents that I asked a company principal that he be assigned permanently to work on my project team. I became his mentor. I was only a dozen years older than he was.

We worked together like the master and apprentice in the medieval craft guilds of olde England. I passed on everything I knew to him as time went by. On some projects I would send him out to the construction site to appreciate the reality of the lines he drew on paper. Later on I would send him to attend the project meetings between the Contractors and our Clients as our company representative. He was in his mid 20's by then and he thrived on the challenges of the higher responsibilities he was given. He never shirked from them, in fact he kept asking for more.

After several years, he assumed the leadership of my project team. With his acquired knowledge and varied experience it was his turn to mentor the young graduate architects who joined our team. He would explain the details of the projects with them and tell them what are needed to be done. Though a young black man with just a high school education he completely earned their respect and trust. Over time he learned the architectural profession upside down and inside out.

In Virginia, as in many US states, someone who has gained ten years of architectural knowledge and experience through work apprenticeship is allowed to take the professional board exams upon the recommendation of the company one worked for. He applied for it, passed the exams, and earned the title of a Registered Architect in the Commonwealth of Virginia.

He left us soon after to join another company as their Chief of Architectural Production. He took charge of all the working drawings for the projects of the firm. He decided on what are needed to be shown and how to show them. He set the standard operating procedures for the company. Just below the level of company principals, he shared equal responsibilities with another architect who was their Chief of Design. He was on his way to becoming a very important man.

Years later he left that firm to join an international architectural-engineering company, with projects all over the world, as the Principal-in-Charge of institutional projects. He supervised his teams of many project managers working on different projects, among them the planned renovations to the Pentagon building. He was the RARE black executive in the rarefied corporate world of white managers.

I have always thought of him as my younger brother. His only son had graduated from college, the first in his family. His father was a laborer in the railroad yards of Alexandria, VA.

We both got to where we wanted to be, not because we were brown, black, white, yellow or red, or because our forebears were subjugated and exploited by the white man. It was the inevitable result of hard work and dedication to learning. We shall overcome. We had overcome!!!

We are the homo sapiens, born of common ancestors, hundreds of thousands of years ago. ignorance, fear, greed and jealousy of our elders have made us hate and kill one another throughout the milleniums. We are all alike, wherever we may be in the world. We are brothers and sisters to each other. We must spread trust, love, compassion and understanding among all peoples of the world. we must turn our backs on hate, fear, greed and jealousy as motivators of our lives. we must become civilized to flourish or together we perish as a specie.

Publisher - Tatay Jobo Elizes
job_elizes@yahoo.com - tatay@usa.com

Writings 1 Book, 2009 + I. **Catch That Story** - *Tatay Jobo Elizes, publisher* + II. **Obit** - *Bambi Harper, Famous columnist* + III. **Speech, UP, 2003** - *Butch Jimenez, PLDT Executive* + IV. **Speech, Silliman U, 2006** - *Butch Jimenez, PLDT Executive* + V. **The Mission Moment** - *Dr. Phil Stack, Psyhologist* + VI. **Writing Underground** - *Mila D. Aguilar, Poet & Writer* + VII. **Academic Freedom** - *Mila Aguilar, Poet & Writer* + VIII. **Subanon Spirits of Rice & Land** - *Noel Cornel Alegre, Academician* + IX. **I Look Out The Window** - *Atty. Toto Causing, Lawyer, Journalist & Writer* + X. **Ride On A Bus, Poem** - *Anonymous via Melanie Ferrer, Budding Poet* + XI. **Why Am I Doing This** - *Susie Barbieri, Social Activist* + XII. **How To Court A Philipine Lady** - *Rodel Ramos & Jose Torres, Civic Leaders* + XIII. **Inspiring Young Filipino Entrepreneur** - *Lloyd Luna, Motivational Speaker* + XIV. **The Success Story of Ian Del Carmen** - *Lloyd Luna, Motivational Speaker* + XV. **Story of Bacna Surgical Mission** - *Sylvia Salvador, Civic Leader* + XVI. **1987 Philippine Constitution** - *Full Text (Special Feature)* + XVII. **Why Publish Writings** - *Tatay Jobo Elizes, Publisher*

Writings 2 Book, 2009 + I. **Why Can't We Act Up Together** - *Susie Barbieri, Social Activist* + II. **I Know Where They Are All Going** - *Cesar Lumba, Writer & Poet* + III. **There Is Hope For The Philippines** - *Grace Padaca, Isabela Governor* + IV. **Pointers On Employment Abroad** - *Melanie Aquino, Dentist & Writer* + V. **Without KNCHS: (Love story)** - *Atty. Toto Causing, Jury Proponent, Writer* + VI. **422 Years Ago** - *Rodel Rodis, Writer & Political activist* + VII. **Filipino American History Month** - *Rodel Rodis, Writer & Political activist* + VIII. **Love is the Next Truth,**

poem - *Daniel Rodis, son of Rodel* + IX. **A Need For Reflection - Gloom** - *Cesar Torres, Politial Activist, academician* + X. **Our Purpose Driven Life** - *Joey Concepcion, RFM Pres. & GoNegosyo activist* + XI. **Did Ninoy Die For Nothing** - *Joey Concepcion, RFM Head & GoNegosyo Activist* + XII. **Why The Filipino Voted** - *Pablito Lim, Zambales Businessman* + XIII. **Life And Love, Poem** - *Nannette Yatco, Dentist, Fine Artist, Poet* + XIV. **Criteria - American Institute of Philanthropy** - *Charity Guidelines (Feature)* + XV. **Strangers In Our Own Country** - *Casiano Mayor Jr., Author & Writer* + XVI. **Coming Revolution In The Ballot** - *Cesar Lumba, Author & Writer* + XVII. **2009 - A Retrospective** - *Cesar Lumba, Author & Writer* + XVIII. **All Over The World** - *Vicente Rivera Jr., Short Story Writer* + XIX. **Harvest** - *Loreto Paras Sulit, Short Story Writer* + XX. **Things Your Burglar Won't Tell** - *Jude Tagaciudad, Writer* + XXI. **The Gypsy Soul** - *Casiano Mayor Jr., Author & Writer* + XXII. **An End To Cheating** - *Sonny Coloma, Academician & Writer* + XXIII. **Toward Culture of Giving** - *Sonny Coloma, Academician & Writer*

Writings 3 Book, 2010 + I. **EPIC25- Emerging Philippines Investors Coalition**- *Norman Madrid, Economist* + II. **Management Ability As An Issue** - *Dr. Rene B. Azurin, Academician* + III. **Do We Really Want To Give Our Politicos More Power** - *Dr. Rene B. Azurin* + IV. **Will 2010 Fulfill High Hopes For Better Life** - *Ernie D. Delfin, Journalist* +V. **Comelec Is The Root Of All Evils** - *Toto Causing, Journalist, lawyer* + VI. **Advantages of Federalism/Parliamentary** - *Dr. Jose Abueva, Ex-UP President* + VII. **Sometimes A Great Nation** - *Mar-Vic Cagurangan, Journalist* + VIII. **Great Conspiracy** - *Mar-Vic Cagurangan, Journalist* + IX. **Of Speech & Life's Riddles** - *Casiano Mayor, Author, journalist* + X. **Bad Start To The Year** - *Rod Garcia, Lawyer, composer, guitarist, poet* + XI. **A Dinner Out** - *Rod Garcia, Lawyer, composr, guitarist, poet* + XII. **One More Time** - *Roy Gaane, Writer* + XIII. **Musings** - *Ceres Busa, Writer* + XIV. **Value Formation For Good Citizenship** - *Roger Reyes* + *JMC Nepomuceno* + *Ramon Gonzales* + *CDVictory* + *Mila Marzon, writers* +XV. **On Being Filipino American** - *John Reyes, Writer* + XVI. **The Monterey Peninsula** - *John Reyes, Writer* + XVII. **The Salaza Fiesta** - *John Reyes, Writer* + XVIII. **Salawikain: Filipino Proverbs** - *John Reyes, Writer* + XIX. **Musikero (The Musician)** - *John Reyes, writer* + XX. **Strange Noises** - *Tatay Jobo Elizes, Publisher*

Writings 4 Book, 2010 + I. **The State of Our Nation and Democracy In 2010: Building 'The Good Society" We Want** *Dr. Jose V. Abueva, University President* + II. **Assessing Expanded Role of AFP in Nation Building** - *Col. Dennis Acop, Ret.* + III. **Assessing RP's Security Strategies Alternative Views** - *Col. Dennis Acop, Ret.* + IV. **The Way We Were** - *Fred Natividad, Accountant & Writer* + V. **Veterans of Ipo Dam, A**

Letter - *Tony Meloto, GK Fiunder* + VII. **The Scent of Hope For The Global Filipino** - *Tony Meloto, GK Founder* + VIII. **Fleshing Out The Broad Strokes** - *Felicito (Tong) C. Payumo, Former Cong.* +IX. **In Search Of Leaders (Part1)** - *Felicito (Tong) C. Payumo, Ex-Cong./SBMA Chair.* + X. **In Search of Leaders (Part 2)** - *Felicito (Tong) C. Payumo* + XI. **A Conspiracy of Dunces** - *Cesar Lumba, Writer, Blogger* + XII. **Only Science Can Solve Poverty** - *Flor Lacanilao, Scientist-Academician* + XIII. **Education Reform Amid Scarcity** - *Flor Laconia* + XIV. **Highblood: Obituaries/Reasons** - *Flor Laconia* + XV. **How Money Works** - *Edmund Lao, Writer* + XVI. **State of Economy & Society, 2002** - *Juan Dela Cruz - Txtmania.com* + XVII. **Global Filipinos** - *Juan Dela Cruz - Txtmania.com* + XVIII. **Understanding Poverty** - *Juan Dla Cruz - Txtmania.com* +XIX. **Kuyakuy** - *Dr. Ramon Marquez, Practicing Doctor* + XX. **Cambodian Octopus** - *Joey Jamito, Writer* + XXI. **Inspite Of Herself, I Still Love The Philippines** - *Joey Jamito* + XXII. **Love Has Wings** - *Percy Campoamor Cruz - Story Teller, writer* + XXIII. **Walk For Kris** - *Rod Garcia - Lawyer, writer, music, guitarist* + XXIV. **Coldblooded, But** + **Alive** - *Rod Garcia* + XXV. **It Takes A Village** - *Rod Garcia* = XXVI. **Beauty Contest** - *Rod Garcia* + XXVII. **Eight Points In Enlightening The Elites** - *Orion Perez Dumdum, writer* + XXVIII. **Case Against "Cellphone Revolution"**- *Sarah Raymundo, writer, activist*

Writings 7 Book, 2010 - My Vintage Pics - Pictorials, Tatay Jobo Elizes

Writings 8 Book, 2010 + I. **The Church and the State: In Search of Common Ground** - *Gel Santos Relos* + II. **President Aquino:** "Walang Kaibigan, Walang Kamag-anak" - *Gel Santos Relos* + III. **What Makes Us "Pinoy"** - *Gel Santos Relos, TV Host, Writer* + IV. **Minsan may Isang Puta (2007)** - *Mike Portes, Writer, IT expert* + V. **Build Our Dream** - *Jose Ma. Montelibano, Columnist* + VI. **Hope In Europe** - *Tony Meloto, Gawad Kalinga Founder, Writer* + VII. **Wealth in Canada** - *Tony Meloto* + VIII. **Parenthood: A Sacred Covenant,** *Philip S. Chua, MD, FACS, FPCS* + IX. **Are We, Humans, Really Civilize? (Or, are we for the birds.)** *Philip S. Chua,* + X. **Save Our Nation** - *Philip S. Chua, MD, FACS, FPCS* + XI. **A Time To Pause** - *Philip S. Chua, MD, FACS, FPCS* + XII. **The Gawad Kalinga Virus** - *Philip S. Chua, MD, FACS, FPCS* + XIII. **A Marching Order For P-Noy** - *Philip S. Chua, Chair, Fil United Netw., USA* + XIV. **"Bayan Ko" Bonds** - *Philip S. Chua, Chairman, Filipino United Network - USA*+ XV. **P-Noy's First 99 Days** - *Philip S. Chua, Chairman, Filipino United Network-USA* + XVI. **The Practice of Quackery in the Phils.** - *Cesar D. Candari, MD, FCAP Emerit.* + XVII. **Remember When? A Brief History of Old and Recent Past** - *Cesar Candari* + XVIII. **The Philippines Before and What Now?** - *Cesar D. Candari, MD, FCAP Emeri* + XIX. **The Traffic Problems are Beyond "Wang-Wang"** -*Cesar D.*

Candari, MD, FCAP + XX. **Behind The Gold** - Eliseo Serina, MD + XXI.
May Angal? (Any Complaint?) - Greg B. Macarena + XXII. **Pagbalik-
Tanaw Sa Kapatirang Masoneriya Sa Pilipinas** - Irineo P. Goce + XXIII.
Mysteries & Riddles Behind RP's Corridors Of Power - Irineo P. Goce +
XXIV. **Wika - Diwa Ng Lahi, O - Ang Tore ni Babel Sa Pilipinas** - Irineo
P. Goce + XXV. **Can There Be Peace? Is There Hope For Progress?** -
Irineo P. Coce + XXVI. **Drama Queen** - Percival Campoamor Cruz, Writer +
XXVII. **Ang Tulay na Kahoy** - Percival Campoamor Cruz, Writer + XXVIII.
Sa Alaala ni Maria Lorena Barros - Percival Campoamor Cruz, Writer +
XXIX. **Text Game or Text Gambling?** - Juan dela Cruz + XXX. **Of
Husbands and Wives** - Juan dela Cruz + XXXI. **It Must Be Love** - Juan
dela Cruz + XXXII. **Elite Triad Blocking Reform** - Demosthenes B.
Donato

Writings 9 Book, April 2011+ I. **Solidarity in Literature W/out
Borders** - Simeon Dumdum Jr + II. **Macario Sakay Vindicated . . .**-
Gemma Cruz Araneta + III. **The Dilemma of the Last Filipino** - Larry
Henares + IV. **Ping Joaquin, Fil. Jazz Pianist, my Father** - Tony
Joaquin +V. **Bert Del Rosario - Inventor - Sing-Along** - Tony Joaquin +
VI. **Xmas Article 2009** - Allen Gaborro, writer + VII. **Beaches (short
story)** - Allen Gaborro + VIII. **Democracy Versus Discipline** - Allen
Gaborro + IX. **Amend the Const. Make Jury Trial** - *Atty.* Toto C. Causing
+ X. **Dakdak Beach Resort in Dapitan City** - Toto C. Causing + XI. **So
I'm Dark-skinned, Leave Me Alone** - Mar-Vic Cagurangan + XII. **Dig My
Sexy Flip Accent, Arizona** - Mar-Vic Cagurangan + XIII. **A Fan Mail
From Prison** - Mar-Vic Cagurangan, journalist + XIV. **Three Poems: a.
Please Don't Let Her Know, b. I Have Memories of My own, c. God
Has Made Someone Only For me** - Emily Espanol Derry + XV. **Three
Love Poem: a. Some Good Things Never Last b. The Dance c. As I
Trod Upon Your Ground** - Elyn Jean Felarca + XVI. **My Advocacy** -
Naysan A. Albaytar, writer + XVII. **Feminism: The Great Paradox** - Laura
Wade, blogger + XVIII. **A Blast From the Past** - Peter Allan Mariano,
writer + XIX. **Bus. Perspective: Bldg. Your Future** - Peter Allan Mariano
+ XX. **An Overview of Health Connections** - Peter Allan Mariano + XXI.
My Workspace At Home - Marge Trajeco-Aberásturi, writer + XXII.
Investing on a Home Business - Marge Trajeco-Aerator + XXIII. **A
Brighter Day for Little Jane** - Julia Carreon-Lagoc, journ + XXIV. **A
Consummation Devoutly to Be Wished** - Julia C. Lagoc + XXV. **No Birds
and Beetles and Trees** - by Julia Carreon-Lagoc + XXVI. **Ang Wika - Ang
Tore Ni Babel Sa Pilipinas** - Irineo Goce + XXVII. **Scattered Thoughts** -
Anonymous

Solo Authored Books: + Book A - **Turning Points - Empty
Dreams** - Job Elizes Sr,1968 (Reissue 2009) + Book B - **Be Considerate** -

Behaviour Issues - *Tatay Jobo Elizes (Jr), 2009* + Book C - **Piglets Unlimited - Wealth Untapped** - *Tatay Jobo Elizes, 2009* + Book D - **Out of the Misty Sea We Must** - *Cesar Lumba. 2010* + Book E - **Fulfilled** - *Gonzales Reynaldo, Editor, 2010* + Dook F - **Reflections** - *Bert Guiang, 2010* + Book G - **Writings 7 - My Vintage Pics** - *Tatay Jobo Elizes, 2010* + Book H - **May Bagwis Ang Pag-ibig** - *Percival* Book I - **Letters To Matrimony** - *Irineo Perez Coce, Ka Pule2, 2011* + Book J - **Songs I Wish You Knew** - *Soledad R. Juan, 2011* + Book K - **Make My Day** - *Larry Henares Jr., 1993, Re-issue 2011* + Book L - **Our Guerrero Family** - *Tatay Jobo Elizes*

"Buy online and Gift Somebody - paperback or kindle edition"